How To Make
NUCLEAR
WEAPONS
OBSOLETE

HOW TO MAKE
NUCLEAR
WEAPONS
OBSOLETE

ROBERT JASTROW

LITTLE, BROWN AND COMPANY · BOSTON · TORONTO

LIBRARY OF CONGRESS CATALOG CARD NO. LC 85-40395

FIRST EDITION

Portions of this work have appeared in *Commentary, The New York Times* and *Science Digest.*

Published simultaneously in Canada
by Little, Brown & Company (Canada) Limited

PRINTED IN THE UNITED STATES OF AMERICA

To the men and women who want to see nuclear weapons disappear from the face of the earth.

Contents

Illustrations

Acknowledgments

Research based on the new technologies of missile defense—the ultra-compact computer, the laser and other sophisticated devices—offers the promise of an end to the nuclear nightmare. How these technologies work, and how they can deliver us from the menace of nuclear destruction, make a fascinating story of scientific and technical accomplishment. I am grateful to many friends at Los Alamos, Livermore and in the Department of Defense who have shared with me some of their technical knowledge of the new developments on an unclassified level. I am particularly indebted to Dr. Gregory Canavan of the Los Alamos National Laboratory, Dr. Lowell Wood of Lawrence Livermore National Laboratory, and Major Simon P. Worden of the Department of Defense, who have given generously of their time in many long discussions and meetings over a period of more than a year. I have also profited greatly from conversations with General James A. Abrahamson of the Department of Defense, Dr. Christopher Cunningham of Livermore Laboratory, Dr. O. Judd of Los Alamos, and Ronald R. Sigismonti of the General Electric Company.

I should like to express my appreciation to Gregory Fossedal for many interesting conversations on missile defense. My debt to *The Abolition* by Jonathan Schell is very great.

This book could not have come into being without the invaluable support of my colleague, Mrs. Doris Cook. Her gifts of a fine sense of language and an exceptional lucidity of thought have greatly improved the clarity of the book.

My editor, Beth Rashbaum, and my long-time friend and associate, Lisl Cade, made many valuable suggestions in regard both to content and to clarity. I should also like to thank Kathleen Dolan for the preparation of the index, and Angela Kukoda for a careful reading of the manuscript and the proofs.

Part I: Defending Against Missiles

1 A New Strategic Vision

Not many people know that for thirteen years the official policy of the United States government has been to keep the American people defenseless against Soviet nuclear attacks. But this is the case. Thirteen years ago the United States and the Soviet Union signed a treaty — the so-called Anti-Ballistic Missile treaty or ABM treaty — which says that each country guarantees to keep its people undefended against a nuclear attack by the other side.

Most people are incredulous when they hear this. Yet the language of the treaty is plain. It states:

> "Each party [that is, the US or the USSR] undertakes not to deploy ABM systems for defense of the territory of its country and not to provide a base for such defense."

There is no quarreling with the intent of that statement. It says that the governments of the US and the USSR have entered into a solemn written agreement to keep their countries undefended against nuclear attacks. The agreement was ratified by the Congress in 1972 and has been the law of the land ever since.

Why did our government promise to keep its people naked before the threat of nuclear destruction? How could an American president sign away the right of self-defense of the American people? That makes no sense on the face of it. Yet there is a certain logic to the idea. According to the reasoning of the officials who worked out the ABM treaty, if both superpowers leave themselves undefended, the Soviets know that when they launch a missile attack against us, our own missiles will lay waste their homeland in reprisal. And, of course, we know that if we attack the Soviet Union, our nation will be destroyed by Soviet missiles. This knowledge deters both countries from starting a war, and makes for a very stable situation.

If, however, either side ever acquires an effective defense against enemy missiles, it can attack the other side with impunity, secure in the knowledge that its defense would protect it from retaliation.

The officials who devised this strategy called it Mutual Assured Destruction because it assures the destruction of both nations if either one makes a mistake. Sometimes the idea is known as the MAD strategy because of its initials. The defense of the US against Soviet missiles has rested on this strategy for two decades.

When President Reagan came into office, he was troubled by the inhumanity of the policy of Mutual Assured Destruction. Because of this doctrine, he could, if informed that Soviet missiles are on their way, be required to issue an order that would reduce millions of Soviet civilians to charred corpses. "To rely on the specter of retaliation," the President said, "is a sad commentary on the human condition."

That brief statement contains the essence of the moral dilemma posed by the doctrine of MAD. This doctrine, although invented by intellectuals who probably have never killed a fellow human, is, nonetheless, a cruel policy, because it leaves the American people open to incineration by Soviet

14

nuclear weapons, and only offers the incineration of the Soviet people as a deterrent to that dreadful act.

President Reagan decided that there must be a better way to protect the United States from the danger of a nuclear attack. In his "Star Wars" speech of March 23, 1983, he offered a new strategic vision to the American people. The policy he had inherited from his predecessors depended on the threat of killing millions of Soviet civilians as the main deterrent to a Soviet nuclear attack on our country. President Reagan proposed to turn away from this policy. "The human spirit," he said, "must be capable of rising above dealing with other nations by threatening their existence." And the President called on our scientists to devise a means of intercepting and destroying the attacking missiles and their warheads in mid-flight. Let us go back to the old-fashioned, reliable kind of defense, he said — a defense that puts a shield between the United States and its enemies to protect us from their deadly weapons.

Some scientists objected to this proposal. They said that because of the great destructive power of nuclear weapons, a defense against missiles must be perfect to be useful, and a perfect defense is, of course, unattainable. But this reasoning is flawed. Suppose our defense is 80 percent effective — a very conservative estimate, according to defense experts. That means we can shoot down 4 out of 5 of Soviet warheads in a mass attack. With such a defense in place the Soviets will know that the bulk of our nuclear missile forces will survive their attack. They will know that if they attack us, we will be able to strike back with our nuclear weapons and reduce all the major Soviet cities to rubble in thirty minutes.

The Soviets will know this, and they will not attack us if we have an 80 percent defense against their missiles, or even a 60 or 70 percent defense. Our defense need only be good enough to guarantee the survival of most of our retaliatory forces — the key missile silos, Trident submarine pens, air bases — and, most important of all, the chain of command, beginning

15

with the President, that would actually order a nuclear counterattack against the Soviet Union.

Such a defense, preserving the destructive power of our nuclear arsenal, will virtually foreclose the option of a first strike by the Soviet leaders. Its deployment will serve notice on the Soviet leadership that it cannot hope to decapitate our political and military command and eliminate or greatly reduce our power of nuclear retaliation. In these circumstances, a nuclear first strike by the Soviet Union will necessarily seem to Soviet leaders to be a suicidal act.

That fact will deter the Soviet leaders from planning an attack. By deterring the Soviet leaders from an attack, our defense will protect the people of America from destruction.

2 The Threat

When the United States signed the ABM treaty, our arms control experts thought they had a firm commitment from the Soviet Union to exercise restraint and not add too many missiles to its nuclear arsenal.* The idea was that it would be all right for the United States to give up its defenses and rely on the threat of retaliation to deter an attack, as long as the Soviets did not have enough power in their nuclear arsenal to wipe out our retaliatory forces with a surprise blow. If they developed that much power, then the whole theory of the ABM treaty and Mutual Assured Destruction would collapse like a house of cards.

But no sooner was the ABM treaty signed, than the Soviets proceeded to build up their missile forces to an awesome level. They built and deployed an entire generation of ICBMs — the so-called "fourth generation" — that were bigger, more

---

*Our negotiators felt so strongly about this point that they wrote a so-called "unilateral understanding" into the treaty, which said that one of the main objectives of the negotiation was "to reduce . . . threats to the survivability of our respective strategic retaliatory forces."

destructive, and more accurate than their previous models. The warheads on these missiles were accurate enough to destroy our hardened, i.e., heavily protected, missile silos and other key military sites. By 1980, Soviet missile strength had reached the point where a surprise attack by the Soviets could eliminate a large part of our missile force and cripple our power to retaliate against their attack. That knocked the stuffing out of Mutual Assured Destruction. The result was a nightmare for American security. Our adversary had created a great force for the destruction of the military power of the United States, and we had signed away the right to defend ourselves.

One of the fourth-generation Soviet missiles, the SS-18, is twice as big as an MX missile, and presently carries 10 nuclear warheads with an explosive power of five megatons.* A single SS-18 can be loaded with as many as 30 warheads. At last report, the USSR had 308 monster SS-18s in the field. The Soviet Union also has in the field 360 missiles of the new type known as the SS-19, each as large as an MX missile. The SS-18s and SS-19s carry a total of more than 5000 accurate warheads with a capability for destroying missile silos and other critical targets in the United States. The megatonnage, or power for destruction, residing in just these two types of Soviet missiles — the SS-18 and the SS-19 — is far greater than the megatonnage of the entire U.S. missile and bomber force. All this has happened since the signing of the ABM treaty.

And the Soviets have kept on building. They have in the final stages of development four types of "fifth-generation" missiles that are as powerful as the old ones, and even more accurate and deadly against our hardened military sites. Still worse, from the viewpoint of arms control, some of the new

---

*A megaton, the unit of explosive energy commonly used to describe the size of a nuclear warhead, is the energy released by the detonation of a million tons of TNT.

missiles are not fixed in silos. They can be carried around the country on trucks and launched from any place close to a highway. That means they can be concealed from the view of our satellites, so that we cannot verify whether the Soviets are sticking to their side of the arms control agreement.

On April 2, 1984, the Soviets fired a salvo of six SS-20 missiles on a course over the North Pole towards the United States. The missiles were deliberately exploded in flight before their warheads reached us. This test flight suggested that SS-20s may have a double purpose. Nominally targeted against Western Europe and Japan, they have sufficient range — possibly at the cost of eliminating one or two of their three warheads — to reach the United States if fired from Siberia over the Pole.

The USSR has at least 400 SS-20 launchers, all reloadable with up to 5 reloads, according to intelligence reports. Each missile carries two or three warheads, depending on the distance to its target. That means several thousand warheads that might be targeted on missile silos, submarine bases and other military sites in a nuclear first strike, in addition to the 5000 accurate warheads on the SS-18 and SS-19. For comparison, the United States has 900 accurate warheads — the Mark 12A warheads on its Minuteman III missiles — with the accuracy and destructive power needed to damage military targets in the Soviet Union.

It is not clear why the Soviets are continuing to enlarge their huge arsenal of accurate missiles, which already goes far beyond any reasonable level of military power they would need as a deterrent to an American attack. A great deal of money goes into making missiles as accurate as these. That money would be wasted if the Soviets intended their new missiles to be exploded over unprotected cities, as a deterrent to an American attack on Soviet cities. (An attack on cities does not require great accuracy, since the power of a nuclear weapon can destroy a city if the weapon explodes anywhere in the city's vicinity.) Apparently the Soviet leaders are bent on acquiring a different kind of missile force — not one designed to deter an attack on Soviet civilians, but one that can destroy the military power of the United States. They are building a first-strike force.

The new Soviet missiles, with their enormous numbers of highly accurate warheads, are a greater threat to American security than any other weapon in the Soviet arsenal. For twenty years the United States has relied on the three legs of the famous American "strategic nuclear triad" as our means of discouraging the USSR from an attack on the American homeland. The elements of the triad are Minuteman missiles on the land, B-52 bombers in the air, and Poseidon and Trident submarines in the sea. The Minuteman missiles are housed in silos — underground hollow cylinders of reinforced concrete. Most of the warheads on the Soviet ICBMs are sufficiently accurate to land within 250 yards of these missile silos and the underground bunkers that house the men and equipment needed to launch the missiles. The Soviet warheads are also sufficiently powerful to cave in an American Minuteman silo at a distance of 250 yards and destroy it, even if the silo has been "hardened" by tons of concrete and steel. As a result, according, to General John W. Vessey, Jr., Chairman of the Joint Chiefs of Staff, the Soviet Union can now destroy 70 to 75 percent of our Minuteman missiles in a surprise attack.

Moreover, the accuracy of Soviet warheads, which is the key factor in destroying hardened targets, has improved by about a factor of two from one generation of Soviet missiles to the next.* The newest Soviet missiles of the fifth generation,

---

*A twofold gain in warhead accuracy has the same effect on a hardened silo as a tenfold increase in the destructive power of the warhead. Calculations show that if the accuracy of a Soviet warhead improves from 250 yards to 125 yards, the chance of destroying a Minuteman silo jumps from 57 percent to 95 percent.

currently being tested in the Pacific, may be able to eliminate 90 to 95 percent of American ICBMs outright. When to these prospects for the destruction of the missiles themselves are added the potential for destroying, with highly accurate Soviet rockets, the launch-control centers that house the American officers who would press the buttons, and for destroying the communication links from the President that would relay the order to execute the counterattack, the chances for effective retaliation with our ICBMs dwindle to the vanishing point.

The upshot of the matter is that our Minuteman missiles — the land leg of the U.S. strategic triad — are vulnerable to a Soviet attack and becoming more so every year.

The air-based leg of the triad is even more vulnerable to a Soviet surprise attack. Seventy percent of all B-52s are normally not on the alert at any one time, and are likely to be destroyed by Soviet missiles at the outset. Of those escaping few would get across the border of the Soviet Union. Soviet air defenses, comprising over 2,000 fighters, 7,000 radars, and about 10,000 surface-to-air missiles, are the most massive in the world. Our B-52s are antiquated planes, twenty-five years old on the average, and have lots of nooks and crannies in their contours that reflect radar waves strongly and cause the planes to show up clearly on Soviet radars. B-52s also fly at high altitudes on their bombing runs, which means they can be picked up by a radar at a greater distance. Finally, they fly at the slow, subsonic speed of a commercial airliner. As a result, they are easy targets for Soviet fighter-interceptors and surface-to-air missiles. Secretary of Defense Caspar Weinberger reported some years ago, "The aging B-52 G/H bombers will not be capable of effectively penetrating the Soviet air defenses in the mid-1980s."

The air-launched cruise missile is intended to restore the usefulness of the B-52s in the triad. The cruise missile is a pilotless jet aircraft that navigates itself without human assistance, checking its radar signals against a map of the terrain stored in an onboard computer. Cruise missiles do not have an intercontinental range, but they can be carried to the borders of the USSR by B-52s and launched from the air.

Once across the border, the cruise missile is supposed to be able to penetrate Soviet air defenses more effectively than the B-52 because it flies very low, hugging the terrain and staying out of sight of Soviet radars. However, the current version can be shot down by a Soviet SA-10, a relatively new surface-to-air missile. It can also be shot down by the new Soviet Foxhound fighter. The Foxhound, which has the look-down, shoot-down capability needed to intercept a cruise missile, flies at top speed of Mach 2.4 or 1,550 miles per hour. In Soviet tests, a Foxhound at an altitude of 20,000 feet successfully destroyed drone aircraft, imitating American cruise missiles, that were flying at 200 feet. These Soviet developments may explain why the Defense Department has cut its order of air-launched cruise missiles from 4,348 down to 1,499.

Improved cruise missiles — supersonic, and with a "stealth" design making them nearly invisible to Soviet radar — are under development, but will not be available in large numbers before the next decade. Until then, the air-launched cruise missile is not likely to make a major contribution to the viability of the U.S. strategic triad.

The new B-1B bombers, just going into production, will go far toward restoring the effectiveness of the air leg of the triad. The B-1B had been cancelled by President Carter on the ground that the cruise missile made it unnecessary, but the Reagan administration brought it back to life. The B-1B is designed to be considerably less visible to Soviet radar than the B-52. It also flies lower than the B-52 as it penetrates Soviet airspace. Its exact altitude is classified, but has been described as "tree-top level" — so low, in fact, that collisions with power lines are a hazard. In its run through Soviet airspace — the most important part of the flight — the B-1B also flies considerably faster than the B-52 — Mach 0.85 versus Mach 0.55. But Congress has only approved funding for 100 B-1Bs, and even this reduced force will not be fully available until 1987. In the interim, the bomber leg of the triad will be severely compromised by Soviet air defenses.

So, of the three legs of the U.S. triad, two — the land leg and the air leg — are weak, and will remain weak until later in the decade. That leaves the sea leg — the nuclear-missile submarine — as the only fully effective deterrent remaining. For the present, the triad has been reduced to a monad.

That does not seem like a bad idea. The newest submarines have extraordinarily quiet engines, and therefore are very hard to pick up on sonar. They also have a long range that gives them an enormous volume of ocean to hide in; a Trident missile can reach Moscow from anywhere within 40 million square miles of ocean. As a result, submarines on station are essentially undetectable, and can be counted on to survive a Soviet attack. Of course, all American submarines in port, about half the current fleet of 33 boats, will always be an easy mark for Soviet missiles; but the remaining 15 or 20 submarines can safely hide at sea, at least for the present.*

The survivability of the Trident submarine makes it an ex-

---

*Some experts are concerned about a possible Soviet breakthrough in anti-submarine warfare in the course of some years, that would "make the oceans transparent" and reveal the location of submerged submarines. For example, a submarine churns up cold water from depths, creating a cold-water "wake" that is invisible to the eye but can be seen clearly by heat-sensitive instruments on satellites. Submerged submarines may also create a surface wake in the form of disturbances in the sea-state — the irregular pattern of waves and wavelets on the ocean surface. Fine details of the sea-state can also be measured from satellites with new types of radars. The USSR is reported to be pursuing this line of submarine detection actively.

cellent deterrent to a Soviet attack, especially since the warheads carried on a single Trident can destroy every major city in the USSR. Yet even the Trident has problems as a deterrent. One weakness is its limited ability, when submerged, to communicate with the world above. A submerged submarine is hard to reach by radio because radio waves do not penetrate sea water. To receive a message, the submarine must rise up close to the surface of the ocean. But near the surface it leaves a wake, increasing the risk of detection.* If the submarine actually rises to the surface, it becomes visible to Soviet satellites and can be picked off at will.

Perhaps a suspicious submarine captain, observing that his radio links are dead, will take a chance on surfacing to catch a news broadcast or sample the air for radioactivity, but with Soviet planes and radar satellites reconnoitering the oceans continuously, that will be risky. And suppose the captain decides he has reason to fire off his missiles. That will bring a fearsome retaliation from the Soviet Union. Do we want to entrust the fate of the American people to a naval officer out of touch with civilian authorities? Is it our intent to delegate authority for starting World War III that far down the chain of command? The problem is a serious one.

Our submarines have another weakness as a deterrent to a Soviet attack. A missile launched from a submarine is relatively inaccurate, and is not likely to land close enough to

---

*The Navy tries to overcome this handicap in several ways. In one procedure an airplane flies over the water, trailing a long wire, while the submerged submarine reels out a buoy that rides just under the surface of the ocean and picks up the message. Another technique broadcasts messages to the submarine on extremely low radio frequencies, which can penetrate water to a considerable depth. In time of war, all these methods would be more vulnerable to Soviet disruption than communications on the land. The report by the Scowcroft Commission on Strategic Forces concludes that "communication links with submarines, while likely to improve, will still offer problems not present for land-based systems."

a "hardened" or protected target to do it any serious damage. That means that submarine-launched missiles cannot be used against missile silos, command bunkers, or other military installations, which are always "hardened." They are mainly useful for destroying "soft" targets, like cities and people.* But suppose the Soviet Union were to launch an attack against our military sites while avoiding our cities. We would be deterred from launching our submarine missiles against Soviet cities in reprisal, because the USSR would then surely respond by attacking American cities with the full power of its huge arsenal. The result would be a devastating loss of perhaps 100 million American lives, far greater than if we had withheld retaliation. That millions of Soviet civilians also lay dead or dying would not be a gain to the United States. These circumstances severely limit the value of our submarine deterrent.

Many people mistrust this analysis because they feel that a limited Soviet nuclear attack on military targets will produce nearly as many casualties as an attack on cities. But the facts say otherwise. Suppose the Soviet Union were to direct its highly accurate SS-18 and SS-19 rockets against the American forces capable of nuclear retaliation — missile silos, B-52 airfields, submarine bases, nuclear weapon storage depots, and military command posts — while attempting to spare American cities. Since most of those military sites are in sparsely populated areas, civilian casualties in the U.S. would result mainly from radioactive fallout on cities lying downwind. Calculations on the effects of nuclear explosions indicate that casualties in such a Soviet attack on military sites would be

---

*This situation will change when an advanced submarine missile called the Trident 2 comes into use. The new missile has an improved guidance system with the accuracy necessary to destroy some hardened targets in the USSR. But that will not happen until 1990.

very great, between 2 and 14 million according to estimates by the Department of Defense. However, they would be far fewer than the 80 to 170 million deaths that would result from a deliberate Soviet attack on our cities in response to an American attack on Soviet cities. In spite of the enormity of the two disasters, a real distinction exists between them. One case means the possibility of a recovery for the U.S., and the other case means the annihilation of the American people.

How would an American President respond to such a limited attack by the Soviets, with American military power crippled but the cities largely intact? With only our surviving submarines available for retaliation, he would be limited to two options, and both would be painful. In Henry Kissinger's words, "A President could initiate the extermination of tens of millions of people — first Soviet citizens and then our own - or he could give in." The choices, Kissinger concludes, are "suicide or surrender."

It is sometimes said that a "surgical" nuclear attack on our military sites is impossible, because some Soviet warheads are bound to miss their targets by wide margins. In the words of one critic, Soviet missiles "would be falling all over our country." This is not correct. If the accuracy of a warhead is, say, 250 yards, that means that half the warheads will land within a circle of 250 yards, and half will land outside the circle. But the warheads that land outside will still be clustered in the neighborhood of the aiming point.

So, urban areas will not be destroyed accidentally in a Soviet attack against our military sites. But is it possible that the Soviet Union, in planning an attack on the United States, will decide, nonetheless, that its interest is served by the greatest possible devastation? Will the Soviet Union elect, as part of a calculated plan of attack, to explode megaton warheads over American cities? It seems clear that this can never happen. The leaders of the USSR must know that the one action certain to provoke an attack on their cities would be a Soviet attack on American cities. They must know that some elements of our submarine force are bound to survive their surprise attack, and are sure to visit fearful retribution on Soviet civilians for an attack on American civilians.

And such an attack on American cities will be counterproductive for the USSR in other ways as well. At the least, it will reduce Soviet prospects for extracting food, technology, and industrial loot from a subdued America. At worst, it will damage the atmosphere's fragile ozone layer, bring a nuclear winter to the globe, and visit ruin upon the agricultural lands and people of the Soviet Union. The USSR has everything to lose by an attack on American cities, and little to gain.

The essence of the matter is that American submarines are an effective deterrent to a Soviet attack on our cities, but are not a deterrent to an attack on U.S. armed forces. It is a sobering fact that if the USSR should launch a nuclear strike against our military installations, we could do little about it, short of a suicidal strike against Soviet cities, in the current state of disrepair of our strategic triad.

Experts count and recount missile silos, bombers, submarines, warheads, and megatonnage. They argue over whether we still have a kind of parity with the Soviet Union, in spite of the vulnerability of our ICBMs and B-52s. But there can be no argument about one basic fact: Soviet missile power has been growing faster than ours, and has succeeded in placing a large part of the American strategic deterrent at risk. The trend is frightening. If continued, it will lead to the possibility, some years hence, of a preemptive Soviet attack aimed at the total destruction of American military power.

THE LAND-BASED ARSENALS OF THE TWO SUPERPOWERS. Soviet missiles are shown in black; American missiles are white.

The SS-17, SS-18 and SS-19, all deployed since 1974, are the fourth generation of Soviet land-based missiles. The SS-18, largest missile in the world, is 120 feet high, weighs about 240 tons, and can carry 10 to 30 warheads that can be directed against separate targets. The SS-18 is cold-launched —that is, the missile is popped out of its silo and then ignited, reducing damage to the silo and permitting it to be reloaded with spare missiles.

The Minuteman III, deployed in 1970, is the last U.S. ICBM to be built prior to the MX. The MX is half the size of the SS-18 but more accurate, with an average miss distance of about 150 yards compared to 250 yards for the SS-18.

The U.S. Titan—a missile dating back to 1963—is being phased out and is not shown here. Also not shown are two new Soviet missiles of the fifth generation—the SS-X-26 and SS-X-27—which are still in development.

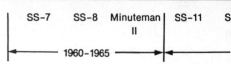

SS-7	SS-8	Minuteman II	SS-11	SS

1960–1965

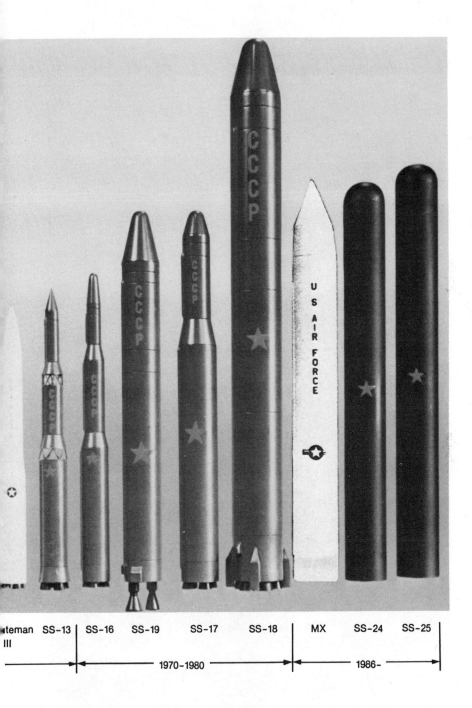

| teman III | SS-13 | SS-16 | SS-19 | SS-17 | SS-18 | MX | SS-24 | SS-25 |

1970–1980   1986-

SILOS. Many Soviet and American land-based missiles are placed in silos—buried structures of heavily reinforced concrete—to protect them from destruction by nearby nuclear explosions. The photograph *below* shows the reinforced structure of steel bars used in a test of a silo designed for the MX missile.

The illustration *below* shows a cutaway of a U.S. Minuteman silo, modified to hold an MX missile. The massive silo door slides open when a launch is imminent. The missile rides on shock-absorbing mounts inside the silo.

The photograph *above* is an aerial view of another
Minuteman launch site, with the silo door closed.
American missile silos are reported to be hardened to
withstand half-megaton nuclear explosions, typical of
Soviet warheads, at a distance of 320 yards or more.
The average miss distance, or circular error probable
(CEP), of the Soviet SS-18 warheads is 250 yards. That
is, half the SS-18 warheads fired in a massive attack will
land within a circle of 250-yard radius around their
targets. The fact that this miss distance is less than the
lethal radius for a Minuteman silo explains why a Soviet
attack could destroy most of our missiles in their silos.

MIRVed MISSILES. Four of the ten warheads carried by the MX missile are shown *below* in an engineering test. Each cone-shaped warhead is approximately six feet high and two feet across at the base. The warheads are sitting on the bus—a structure that can steer itself in space to direct each warhead towards its designated target.

The photograph *opposite* shows the trails of eight MX warheads, launched by a single missile, as they reenter the atmosphere towards the end of their trajectories. Heating by friction, during the rapid passage of the warheads through the atmosphere, causes them to glow brightly.

32

SUBMARINE-LAUNCHED MISSILES. Large nuclear-powered submarines, each carrying 16 to 24 intercontinental ballistic missiles, are the mainstay of the U.S. strategic triad. The Trident submarine (*below*) is nearly three city blocks long and can remain submerged for months at a time.

The photograph at right shows another U.S. ballistic missile submarine of the older Poseidon class with its missile hatches open.

During the launch the missiles are popped out of their tubes by steam pressure and hurled to the surface, where their rocket engines ignite and send them on their way. (*facing page*)

SOVIET MISSILES ON PARADE. New Soviet missiles are often a feature of parades marking the anniversary of the Bolshevik Revolution. The facing page shows two SS-10s, a third-generation missile, during the 1967 anniversary celebration. The photograph below shows the SS-15, the largest mobile Soviet missile displayed publicly.

The SS-20, SS-24 and SS-25 are also mobile and easily concealed—a fact that makes verification of arms control limits on numbers of land-based missiles difficult.

3 The Response

How is the United States to respond to this threat? One way is by "Launch On Warning" — hitting the firing button when signals come from U.S. satellites and radars that the Soviet missiles appear to be on the way. As General Vessey said a few years ago, "The Soviets have no assurance that we will ride out [a nuclear] attack."

But Launch On Warning is a policy of last resort, for it can amplify a false alarm into the beginning of World War III. Our government has been driven to contemplate it only as a measure of its desperation, as it contemplates the growing first-strike capability of the Soviet Union. Yet the President today has no useful options to Launch On Warning — except the unleashing of our submarine-launched missiles on the Soviet cities, reducing them to rubble, but with fearsome consequences for the American people in the Soviet strike against our cities that is certain to follow.

At least, a President has no options unless he decides to ride out the attack after all, and sacrifice the bulk of our land-based missiles. But that would be a difficult decision to make, because our land-based missiles have a unique combination of properties. They are the only leg of our strategic nuclear triad that is both *accurate* and *fast*. They are accurate enough to place at risk the most highly prized assets of the Soviet government — the heavily populated bunkers that shelter its military and political leaders, and the missile silos and other facilities that store its nuclear weapons. And they are fast enough to reach these vital sites in the Soviet Union, and disrupt the execution of a Soviet nuclear attack, less than an hour after the attack starts — soon enough to give Soviet leaders pause about continuing their plan.

Bombers and cruise missiles are sufficiently accurate to destroy vital military targets, but slow. Submarine-launched missiles are nearly as fast as land-based missiles, but too inaccurate to score a direct hit on a protected military target and destroy it.

That leaves our land-based missiles as a vital element of the U.S. deterrent. And it leaves us with Launch On Warning as the only response that can guarantee the United States the use of those missiles in the event of a Soviet attack — an unfortunate consequence of our reliance on the doctrine of Mutual Assured Destruction and the ABM treaty.*

Another response to the Soviet threat would be a massive build-up of our own land-based missile forces, sufficient to match the Soviet ICBM force on equal terms. The MX missile has a warhead accurate enough to serve this purpose — accurate enough that is, to place Soviet command posts and other prime military targets at risk. However, the force of 100 MX missiles proposed by the current administration would not be large enough to balance the Soviet threat, because, with ten warheads per missile, it would place in the field only 1000 warheads. One thousand MX warheads would be insufficient

---

*If it were not for the ABM treaty, the U.S. would have another alternative to Launch On Warning for the protection of its land-based missiles. It could build defenses around its missile silos.

in number to make an appreciable dent in the 4000 or so top-priority Soviet military targets.*

Five hundred MX missiles, carrying 5000 warheads, could do the job. That would be a first-strike force to match the Soviet force, and as menacing a threat to the Soviet Union as its ICBMs are to us. The result would be a Mexican stand-off between two adversaries, each armed to the teeth, and each capable of delivering a knockout blow if it could get in the first punch. This would be a balance of sorts, but it would be unstable. There is a better way, and that is the way President Reagan has chosen.

Suppose a brilliant inventor could devise a method to defend the United States against Soviet ICBMs. Then our own ICBMs — Minutemen and MXs — would no longer be vulnerable to a surprise attack. These ICBMs are accurate enough to destroy many hardened targets in the USSR, including the 1500 hardened leadership centers sheltering the Soviet elite. If our missile silos were defended, Soviet leaders could not eliminate this threat to their existence by knocking out American ICBMs in a preemptive first strike. If nothing else deterred the Soviet leadership from an attack on the United States, that circumstance would certainly do so.

Where can we find this invention? The answer is that we already have it. The basic technologies have been proven, they can be put into use quickly.

The key to these technologies is the miniaturized computer. Extraordinary developments in the miniaturization of computer circuits enable millions of transistors and other electronic components to be packed into a space the size of a thumbnail. As a result, defense technicians now have the means for building elaborate computer brains into a very

---

*1400 missile silos, 1500 leadership bunkers, and about 1000 nuclear weapons storage depots and other top-priority sites.

small missile so that it can steer itself toward its target. This tiny missile with brains is often called "a smart bullet" or "a smart rock". Sensing the target either by its delicate emanation of heat waves, or by its radar reflections, the smart bullet analyzes the product of its senses within its highly capable computer brain, and directs a succession of messages to small rockets arranged around its circumference. Delicate thrusts of these rockets steer the defending missile into the path of the oncoming ICBM warhead. The result is either destruction of the warhead by a direct impact, or an explosion of the smart bullet on impact, releasing a cloud of flying metal fragments. The warhead, moving ten times faster than an artillery shell, tears into the cloud of fragments; the skin of the warhead is punctured in many places; its electronics are disabled; and the nuclear bomb inside it is disarmed.

In essence, the defense consists in tossing a keg of nails into the path of the speeding warhead. What makes this simple defense work is its computer brain.

The smart bullet does not have to destroy the warhead to be effective; it only has to prevent the nuclear weapon inside the warhead from exploding. That happens to be fairly easy, because nuclear weapons do not go off very readily; elaborate arrangements and a great deal of fragile electronics are needed to make one explode. Accordingly, a cluster of high-speed metal fragments will usually be sufficient to disarm the weapon's mechanism.

Emplacements of smart bullets surrounding our key

*When there are only a few targets, and the destruction of each one is very important to the Soviet Union, it can always try to overwhelm our defenses by allotting a large number of warheads to each target. However, by the same token, a few sites, each of enormous value to the United States, can be ringed by exceptionally strong defenses comprised of not one or two but perhaps dozens of mini-missiles or more; and this can be done at acceptable cost to the U.S., because only a limited number of such highly valuable sites exist.

military installations can protect our power of retaliation and remove any thought of a first strike against the United States from the minds of the Soviet leaders. Our missile silos can be protected. The communication lines that connect the President and top military commanders to the Minuteman launch-control centers can be protected. Our bomber airfields and submarine bases can be protected. Just two bases — one in Kings Bay, Georgia, and the other in Bangor, Washington — will support our entire fleet of Trident submarines. If these bases are undefended, half the Trident fleet — the part in port when a Soviet surprise attack occurs — must be written off at the outset. A defense of the Trident bases against Soviet missiles will double the effective strength of the American submarine deterrent. All these measures improve our chance of being able to retaliate against a Soviet attack, and therefore make an attack less likely.

A defense that decreases the vulnerability of our nuclear forces is good. A defense that shielded the American people would be better. Can inventive genius find still another device to accomplish this task as well? Once again, the answer is that we already have the invention. It is called the laser.

A laser is like a searchlight; it produces a beam of light. This beam of light, focused on the metal skin of an ICBM, can burn right through it, just as the light of the sun, focused to a narrow spot by a magnifying glass, can burn through a piece of wood or paper. The difference between a laser beam and an ordinary beam of light is that the ordinary beam spreads out as it leaves its source, so that by the time it has traveled several thousand miles — for example, from a satellite over the Soviet Union to a missile field below — the beam is dispersed over an area several miles in diameter. As a result, the intensity of light in any one part of the beam is too weak to hurt anything.

A laser beam, on the other hand, has the remarkable property that all parts of the beam travel in very closely the same direction, so that the beam does not spread apart as rapidly as an ordinary beam as it travels through space. If the energy in the laser beam is intense enough at its source to burn through the metal skin of a Soviet ICBM, it will be nearly as intense, and still able to burn through metal, after it has traveled thousands of miles.

Laser beams have the advantage that they travel at the speed of light, which is 670 million miles an hour, and can cross a continent in a hundredth of a second. Compared to the speed of laser beams, even an ICBM is slow, and the laser beam has no difficulty in catching up to one and intercepting it. One of the disadvantages of a laser beam is that, being a beam of light, it is blocked by clouds and haze. For that reason, laser guns work best if placed in a space station or satellite, far above the atmosphere. They also have a direct line of sight to the Soviet missile fields from that height. Putting a laser gun in a satellite is a feasible project. It means that several tons of equipment and fuel must be ferried into orbit, but that is not a major difficulty. One shuttle flight can carry up to 33 tons into orbit. The Saturn 5 rocket, which sent the astronauts to the moon, lifted more than 100 tons into orbit and the Soviets are reported to have a rocket ready for use that carries 150 tons into orbit.

Unlike the smart bullet, the laser defense is not inexpensive; it is not yet a proven technology; but it has the promise of destroying the Soviet missiles and their warheads as they rise from their silos.

4 Can It Be Done?

When President Reagan announced his proposal for defending the United States against Soviet missiles, the reactions from scientists and politicians were almost uniformly skeptical. Dr. Richard Garwin, who has had a great deal of experience in defense technology, said, "It won't work." Senator Edward Kennedy said the plan was "misleading" and "reckless" and former Defense Secretary Robert S. McNamara called it "pie in the sky."

But when I first heard the President's speech, I thought he had a pretty good idea. I wrote an article commenting favorably on the proposal, and then, a little later, I traveled to Washington to hear a talk by Dr. George Keyworth, the President's Science Adviser, on the strategic and technical implications in the President's plan.

Since Dr. Keyworth was rumored to have made a major contribution to the thinking behind the "Star Wars" speech, I felt I would be getting an insider's view of the technical prospects for success in this difficult undertaking. That was particularly interesting to me, because several of my fellow physicists had expressed the gravest reservations about the technical feasibility of the proposal. In fact, Dr. Hans Bethe, a distinguished Nobel laureate in physics, had said bluntly, "I don't think it can be done."

Dr. Keyworth started by describing the circumstances that had led to the President's speech. Then he got into the technical areas I had come to hear about. "For more than five months," he told us, "some fifty of our nation's better technical minds have devoted their efforts almost exclusively to one problem — the defense against ballistic missiles." This group of specialists, which included some of the most qualified defense scientists in the country, had concluded that the President's goal was realistic — that it "probably could be done."

"The basis for their optimism," Dr. Keyworth went on, "is our tremendously broad technical progress over the past decade." He pointed specifically to the advances in computers and "new laser techniques." He also mentioned the promising new developments that might enable us to protect the vitally important satellites carrying all this laser weaponry and computing equipment, and prevent the Soviets from knocking these critical satellites out as a preliminary to a nuclear attack on the United States. "These and other recent technical advances," Dr. Keyworth concluded, "offer the possibility of a workable strategic missile defense system."

That was pretty clear language. Defense experts had given the President's proposal a green light on its technical merits. I went back to New York with a feeling that the President's vision of the future — a future in which nuclear weapons would be "impotent and obsolete" — was going to become a reality.

The following month a group of university scientists called the Union of Concerned Scientists came out with a report that flatly contradicted Dr. Keyworth's assessment. According to the panel, an effective defense of the United States against Soviet missiles was "unattainable." The report leveled numerous criticisms at the "Star Wars" proposal. It pointed out, *inter alia*, that thousands of satellites, each costing as much as an aircraft carrier, would be needed to provide a defensive screen; that one of the "Star Wars" devices under consideration would require placing in orbit a satellite weighing 40,000 tons; that the power needed for the lasers and other devices proposed would equal as much as 60 percent of the total power output of the United States; and that, in any case, the Soviets would be able to foil our defenses with a large bag of relatively inexpensive tricks, such as spinning the missile to prevent the laser from burning a hole it it, or putting a shine on it to reflect the laser light.

The signers of the report included physicists of world renown and great distinction. The impact of their criticisms seemed absolutely devastating.

Around the same time, another study of the feasibility of "Star Wars" came out with more or less the same conclusion. According to that report, which had been prepared for the Office of Technology Assessment of the Congress, the chance of protecting the American people from a Soviet missile attack is "so remote that it should not serve as the basis for public expectations or national policy."

These scientific studies, documented with charts and tables, apparently sounded the death knell of missile defense. Scientists had judged the President's proposal and found it wanting.

A few weeks later, I received unclassified summaries of the reports by two blue-ribbon panels which the Defense Department had set up to look into the feasibility of a United States defense against Soviet missiles. These were the documents on which Dr. Keyworth had relied in part for his optimistic appraisal. The reports by the government-appointed consultants were as different from the reports by the university scientists as day is from night. One group of distinguished experts said no fundamental obstacles stood in the way of success; the other group, equally distinguished, said it would not work. Who was right? According to the Union of Concerned Scientists' report, "any inquisitive citizen" could understand the technical issues. I decided to look into the matter. This is what I found.

Missiles usually consist of two or three separate rockets or "stages," also called boosters because they boost the payload into space. On top of the uppermost stage sits a "bus" carrying the warheads. One by one, the stages ignite, burn out, and fall away. After the last stage has burned out and departed, the bus continues upward and onward through space. At this point it begins to release its separate warheads. Each warhead is pushed off the bus in a different direction with a different velocity, so as to reach a different target. The missiles with this capability are said to be MIRVed (MIRV stands for multiple independently targetable reentry vehicle).

The best time to attack the Soviet missile is during its so-called "boost phase," while the rocket is still burning, because then the bus with its multiple warheads is still attached and we get all the warheads with one shot. But destroying the missile at this stage is a very difficult task technically, and has provoked a lot of scientific discussion. How can we destroy a Soviet missile thousands of miles away, within seconds or minutes after it has left its silo?

At the present time, one of the most promising technologies for doing that is the laser, which shoots a bolt of light at the missile as it rises. Missiles move fast, but light moves faster. A laser beam travels a thousand miles in less than a hundredth of a second. Focused in a bright spot on the missile's skin, the laser beam either burns a hole through the thin metal of the skin, which is only about a tenth of an inch thick, or it softens the metal sufficiently so that it ruptures and the missile disintegrates.

Now for an important point: to be effective, the laser must have unobstructed views of all the Soviet missile fields. One of the best ways of achieving that is to put the device that produces the laser beams on a satellite and send it into orbit.

So, this, then, is the essence of the plan for a boost-phase defense against Soviet missiles: a fleet of satellites, containing equipment that generates laser beams, circles the earth, with enough satellites in the fleet so that several satellites are over the Soviet missile fields at all times — a sufficient number to shoot down, in the worst case, all 1400 Soviet missiles if they are launched against us simultaneously.

This plan for defending the United States against Soviet missiles seems very promising. Yet the report by the Union of Concerned Scientists says it has absolutely no practical value. This report shows that because of the realities of satellite orbits, the satellites needed to protect the United States against Soviet attack would "number in the thousands." The report's detailed calculations put the precise number at 2400 satellites.

Now everyone acknowledges that these satellites are going to be extremely expensive. Each one will cost a billion dollars or more — as much as an aircraft carrier. Satellites are the big-ticket items in the plan for a space-based defense. If thousands are needed, the cost of implementing the plan will be many trillions of dollars. A defense with a price tag like that is indeed a "turkey," as a spokesman for the Union of Concerned Scientists called it.

If the numbers put out by the Union of Concerned Scientists were right, there would be no point in looking into the plan further. But after the report by the Union of Concerned Scientists hit the papers, I began to hear rumors from professionals in the field that the numbers were not right. The experts had been looking at this problem for more than 10 years, and the accurate results were well known. According to careful computer studies done at the Livermore laboratory, 90 satellites could suffice, and if the satellites were put into low-altitude orbits, we might get by as few as 45 satellites.*

*These numbers depend on the power of the laser beams and the size of the mirror used to focus them. All the studies described here make the same assumptions — a 20- or 25-million-watt-laser and a 30-foot mirror.

So the bottom line is that 90 satellites — and perhaps somewhat fewer — are needed to counter a Soviet attack. That cuts the cost down from many trillions of dollars to a level that could be absorbed into the amount already earmarked by the government for spending on our strategic forces during the next 10 or 15 years. It removes the aura of costliness and impracticality which has been cast over the President's proposal by the Union of Concerned Scientists' report.

The scientists who did these calculations for the Union of Concerned Scientists had exaggerated the number of satellites by a factor of about 25. How did they make a mistake like that? A modicum of thought should have indicated that "thousands" of satellites could not be the right answer. Apparently the members of the panel did begin to think more carefully about the matter later on — but only after they had issued their report — because in testimony before a congressional committee a Union of Concerned Scientists spokesman lowered his organization's estimate from 2400 satellites to 800 satellites.* In a book that came out later, the members of the panel lowered their estimate again, to 300 satellites.** In their most recent publication on the matter, they lowered their estimate once more, to 162 satellites. That was getting closer. Their answer, which started out at 2400 satellites, seemed to be converging to a result in the neighborhood of 100 satellites, which is where the professionals had pegged their results all the while.

*The scientist explained that his panel had forgotten that Soviet missile fields are spread out across a 5000-mile arc in the USSR, and had put all the missiles in one spot. This made it harder for the satellite lasers to reach all the missiles, and meant more satellites were needed.

**The explanation offered by the Union of Concerned Scientists for this correction is that its experts belatedly realized some satellites are closer to their missile quarry than others, and can polish the missile off in a shorter time. That means each satellite can kill more missiles, and therefore, fewer satellites are needed to do the job.

Unfortunately, the Union of Concerned Scientists never said to the press or the Congress: "We have found important mistakes in our calculations, and when these mistakes are corrected the impact is to cut the cost of the missile defense drastically. In fact, correcting these errors of ours has the effect of making the President's idea much more practical than we thought it was when we issued our report." Months after the publication of the UCS report, the magazine *Science 84*, published by the American Association for the Advancement of Science, was still referring to the need for "2400 orbiting laser stations."

When theoretical physicists joust over ideas, a factor of 2 hardly counts; a factor of 3 matters a bit; factors of 10 begin to be important; factors of 100 can win or lose an argument; and factors of 1000 begin to be embarrassing. In a study of the practicality of the neutral particle beam — a beam of penetrating atoms that disables the Soviet missile by scrambling its electronic circuits — the panel of the Union of Concerned Scientists made a mistake by a cool factor of 1600. As in the case of the panel's estimate of the size of our satellite fleet, the direction of its error was such as to make this very promising Star Wars technology seem hopelessly impractical.

According to the scientists who wrote the Union of Concerned Scientists report, the neutral particle beam will be generated by a device called a linear accelerator that will weigh 40,000 tons. To be effective, this enormous weight will have to be placed in a satellite. Of course, the idea of loading 40,000 tons onto an orbiting satellite is absurd. By comparison, the NASA space station will weigh about 40 tons. This finding by the Union of Concerned Scientists made it clear that the plan to use the neutral particle beam is ridiculous.

But the Union of Concerned Scientist's study panel made a mistake. The correct result for the weight of the linear accelerator is 25 tons, and not 40,000 tons. Now, 25 tons is quite a practical weight to put into an orbiting satellite. It is, in fact, about the same as the payload carried in a single flight of the NASA shuttle.*

A Union of Concerned Scientists spokesman admitted his organization's rather large error in congressional testimony shortly after the report came out. But when he made the admission he did not say: "We have made a mistake by a factor of more than a thousand, and the correct weight of the accelerator for this neutral partical beam is not 40,000 tons, but closer to 25 tons." He said, according to the stenographic transcript of the hearing, "We proposed to increase the area of the beam and accelerator, noting that would make the accelerator unacceptably massive for orbital deployment. Our colleagues have pointed out that the area could be increased after the beam leaves the small accelerator."**

Now, this technical language does not convey to a senator attending the hearing that the scientist has just confessed to a mistake which changes a 40,000-ton satellite into a 25-ton satellite. There is nothing in the remark to indicate that a panel of scientists has reached a false conclusion on one of the best Star Wars defenses because the panel made a major error in its calculations.

The report prepared for the Office of Technology Assess-

---

*The shuttle's payload is 33 tons in the orbits currently in use. It would be about 20 tons in the orbits needed for the defensive screen against Soviet missiles.

**Hearings before the Senate Committee on Armed Services, April 24, 1984. According to a spokesman of the Union of Concerned Scientists, the written testimony prepared for the hearing included the phrase, "saving a great deal of weight." However the transcript of the testimony presented at the hearing does not contain this phrase. Even if the phrase had been in the transcript, it would not have conveyed the full flavor of the difference between 25 tons in orbit and 40,000 tons in orbit; but in any event, it is not there.

ment also made a mistake on the neutral particle beam, but this mistake is only by a factor of 15. According to the report, the Soviet Union can protect the electronics in its missiles and warheads from the neutral particle beam with a lead shield about one-tenth of an inch thick. The shield, the report states, would not weigh too much and therefore could be "an attractive countermeasure" for the Soviets.

But scientists at Los Alamos have pointed out that a layer of lead one-tenth of an inch thick will not stop the fast-moving atoms of the neutral particle beam; they will go right through it. In fact, a table printed in the Office of Technology Assessment report itself shows that the lead shield must be 15 times thicker — at least 1-½ inches thick — to stop these fast-moving particles.

A layer of lead as thick as that, wrapped around the electronics in the missile and its warheads, would weigh many tons — considerably more than the total weight of all the warheads on the missile. If the Soviets were unwise enough to follow the advice offered in the report to the Office of Technology Assessment, their missile would be so loaded down with lead that it would be unable to get off the ground.

That would be a great plus for American security, and a nice response from our defense scientists to the President's call for ways of making the Soviet missiles "impotent and obsolete."

Part II: How It Works

5 Satellites

In the third book of his great work, *The Mathematical Principles of Natural Philosophy*, Isaac Newton included a figure intended to explain the motion of the moon in its orbit. The figure shows a cannon on a mountain top with its barrel oriented in a horizontal direction. When a ball is fired from the cannon, it moves forward under the impetus of the pressure exerted by the hot gases in the barrel. At the same time it moves downward under the pull of gravity. The combination of the forward motion and the motion downward under gravity is a curved path, which terminates when the cannonball hits the ground.

If the charge of explosives is increased, the forward velocity increases and the ball traverses a greater distance before it is pulled to the ground by gravity. It is conceivable that a cannon could be constructed of such power that the ball would travel around the earth without striking the ground. The combination of the forward motion produced by firing the cannon, and the downward deflection produced by gravity, would curve the path of the projectile into an orbit circling the earth.

Newton constructed his thought-experiment to explain the

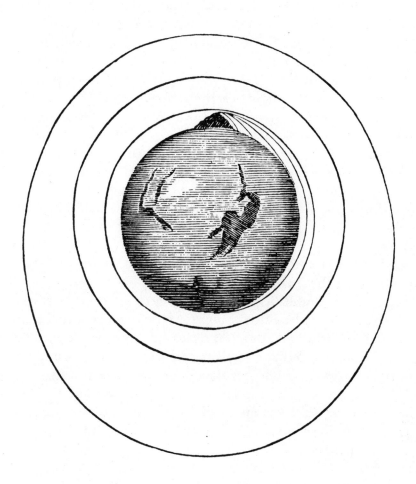

Newton's diagram illustrating the motion of the moon, from the third volume of Principles of Natural Philosophy. *The cannon placed on a mountaintop fires a shot that travels a curved path, compounded of its horizontal forward velocity and a downward motion produced by the gravitational attraction of the earth.*

motion of the moon in its orbit, but it also explains the motion of artificial satellites. A satellite is an object which has been given a forward speed so great that, although falling freely toward the earth at all times, nonetheless it travels entirely around the globe without reaching the ground.

A very high speed — about 17,000 miles an hour or a little less than five miles a second — is necessary to put a satellite into orbit. If the satellite is launched with a lower speed, it will fall back and strike the ground.

In addition to being given a very high forward speed, the satellite must also be lofted to a very high altitude. Theoretically, a satellite could be put into an altitude that skims over the surface of the earth at treetop level. However, the friction produced by the satellite's rapid motion through the relatively dense air of the lower atmosphere would burn it up before it completed one orbit. It turns out that satellites must be placed in orbits at altitudes of 100 miles or more to prevent that from happening. At a height of 100 miles the atmosphere is sufficiently rarefied so that a satellite can orbit the earth a number of times without being destroyed by atmospheric heating.

A satellite orbit at a height of 100 miles is called a low-altitude orbit. It takes about 90 minutes for a satellite in a 100-mile orbit to go around the earth once. Satellites in orbits at higher altitudes travel more slowly, and they also have further to travel. As a consequence they take more time to go around once.* The moon, which circles the earth at an "altitude" of 232,000 miles, takes a full month for an orbit.

Between the 90-minute orbit of a low-altitude satellite and the one-month orbit of the moon, there must be a satellite orbit whose time around the earth is exactly 24 hours. The altitude required for a 24-hour orbit turns out to be 23,000

---

*If a satellite is in a high-altitude orbit, the pull of the earth's gravity is weaker. Therefore a smaller forward velocity will suffice to keep the satellite from hitting the ground.

miles. Twenty-four hour orbits are particularly interesting for practical applications of satellites, because a satellite in such an orbit turns around the earth as fast as the earth turns on its axis. Moving in synchronism with the earth, it hovers over one point on the earth's surface at all times.

A 24-hour orbit is said to be "geosynchronous". Communications satellites are usually placed in geosynchronous orbits; for example, several geosynchronous satellites hover over the center of the Atlantic Ocean, connnecting Europe and America. If these satellites were in any other kind of orbit, they would be over distant places like China part of the time and not very useful for transatlantic communications.

Geosynchronous satellites also have important military uses. They carry three quarters of the military communications of the United States. They also spot the launches of Soviet missiles by looking for the flames of their rocket from orbits that provide a continuous watch over the Soviet missile fields. One so-called Early-Warning satellite hovers over the Indian Ocean, watching for signs of missiles launched from the Soviet Union and China. Two other satellites, over South America and the Pacific Ocean keep watch for missiles launched from submarines. These satellites only give us a thirty-minute warning — the time it takes a missile to cross from the Soviet Union to the United States — but that is better than no warning at all.

The U.S. Early-Warning satellites in orbit right now can tell approximately how many Soviet missiles are launched in an attack and the general area they came from. The next generation of Early-Warning satellites will be much more accurate. They will pinpoint the silos the Soviet missiles were launched from, so that we can avoid wasting our warheads on empty silos when we retaliate. The new models will also indicate which American silos clusters the attacking Soviet warheads are headed for, so that we will have the opportunity to fire our own missiles before they are destroyed.

Satellites have many other military uses in addition to watching for missile launches. Some American military satellites in very low orbits have cameras and television equipment to monitor military and industrial activities in the USSR. They check the production of Soviet tanks and planes, the movement of Soviet troops, and the locations of Soviet missile silos, submarine bases and military air fields. They can tell where nuclear warheads are stockpiled and how much floor space is devoted to research by Soviet scientists on the development of new kinds of nuclear warheads. The satellites look for signs of secret new weapons factories, and concealed missiles, and the special fuehrer-bunkers designed to protect the Soviet elite from American retaliation in the event of a Soviet attack.*

Some U.S. military satellites dip well below 100 miles for a close look at particularly important sites. They can see the palm of your hand from space, and their photographs and television images are nearly sharp enough to read the license plates on cars in Red Square. However, opportunities for good photographs are relatively rare. The best photographs are taken on cloudless days around 11:00 AM, but Eastern Europe is covered with clouds two-thirds of the time, and in the USSR our satellites can photograph the surface on only one or two days each month during the spring and summer. The newest U.S. satellites can form images in infrared light, which means that they will be able to take some photographs at night. These photographs will help to unmask Soviet missile tests which have been conducted under cover of darkness. U.S. satellites also are experimenting with a new type of radar that can form sharp images of terrain completely covered by clouds.

---

*The Soviet government has constructed more than 1500 super-hardened bunkers, located away from urban areas and with their own communications, for 175,000 Soviet leaders and senior civil servants.

Still other American military satellites are equipped with sensitive electronic instruments designed to listen in on all kinds of Soviet radio communications. These satellites are America's ears in space. Their task is not to pick up individual conversations, but mainly to look for changes in "traffic patterns" — for example, the number of messages going back and forth between military headquarters in Moscow and Soviet submarine bases, or between a regional command post and a launch control center. These changes in the intensity of electronic chatter from one part of the Soviet military command to another could betray the final stages in preparation for a nuclear attack on the United States, alerting our forces days or even weeks before the Soviet missile attack actually started.

The electronic satellites also pick up radar signals from the Soviet air defenses and analyze them for holes in the Soviet radar fence. This information could be used by U.S. aircraft, seeking to penetrate the Soviet air defenses, that jam the Soviet radars and spoof them in various ways.

The USSR has its own eyes and ears in space to keep the U.S. under similar surveillance. Soviet forces also use another kind of military satellite that we do not have. This Soviet satellite, called a Rorsat (an acronym for Radar Ocean Reconnaissance Satellite), is equipped with a powerful radar that scans the oceans of the world and pinpoints the locations of U.S. naval vessels. The Soviet radar satellites can keep track of the movements of the ships in our Navy and pass the information on to Soviet bombers and submarines. Some defense experts believe that these satellites have our Navy continually targeted for an attack that could come at any time. The radar-equipped satellites are particularly lethal when combined with another Soviet satellite called the Eorsat (Electronic Ocean Reconnaissance Satellite), that monitors radar and radio transmissions from our ships. The radios can be turned off in a crisis; when the Japanese fleet was steaming to Pearl Harbor it concealed its presence from American forces by maintaining complete radio silence. But there is no way to hide from a satellite equipped with radar.

The Soviet Union has also tested systems for carrying nuclear bombs into orbit. This would permit the Soviet Union to initiate an ICBM attack against the United States from any direction, and not just over the North Pole. It means that the Soviet nuclear weapons can take the long way around the globe to reach their targets, evading our Early-Warning satellites as well as the radar picket fence that faces northward toward the USSR from Alaska and Canada. We would have very little warning of an attack by a bomb-in-orbit — even less than in an ICBM attack — because when the Soviet commander sends the radio signal to the satellite to brake its motion and drop its bomb to the earth, only three or four minutes elapse before the bomb hits the surface.*

The essence of the matter is that the U.S. and the USSR both have placed major military assets in orbit. In fact, today satellites have become as important to military operations as tanks, planes and telephones. As a consequence, control of space — the ability to destroy a potential adversary's satellites and protect one's own — has become a major element in all military planning.

Soviet military planners must have come to that conclusion very early, because nearly twenty years ago the Soviet Union began to work on an antisatellite — a killer satellite — that could destroy other satellites in orbit. The Soviet killer satellite chased after its target in orbit, tracking it with a radar and gradually moving in for the kill. When it was close

*The Soviet Union called the reports on these tests a "fabrication" when Secretary of Defense McNamara first disclosed them. However, the sequence of events in the tests could be seen clearly on U.S. radars. In one case, when the Soviets intentionally exploded their bomb-in-orbit satellite, more than 100 pieces were seen to fly out. In another case, the Soviet bomb-in-orbit test satellite broke up over the United States and deposited fragments across Oklahoma, Kansas and Texas.

enough, the killer satellite detonated a charge of explosives, creating a hail of shrapnel that punctured the skin of the target satellite and destroyed its electronics and other vital parts. Some American scientists have called the Soviet killer satellite crude and ineffective, but actually the version equipped with radar was successful in four of its last five tests and has been an operational system for several years, available for use when needed. The Soviet Union has facilities for launching five killer satellites at one time from a launch center called Tyuratam. That would be enough to blind most of the important U.S. eyes in space at one blow.

A few years ago the Soviets tested a killer satellite in what looked like a rehearsal for a global war. In June 1982, they launched a target satellite, and, shortly after, a killer satellite that chased the target and intercepted it. Next, the Soviets fired two intercontinental missiles from their operational silos, and, almost simultaneously, an SS-20 of the type that is targeted against Western Europe. Then they launched an intercontinental missile from a submarine in the White Sea. Finally, they fired two antiballistic missiles — that is, missiles that destroy missiles — against oncoming warheads that simulate warheads fired by the U.S. in a retaliatory counterattack. All the firings happened in rapid succession within one seven-hour period.

Military experts analyzing this information have concluded that the Soviets were fighting an imaginary nuclear war. The first step was the launch of a killer satellite to simulate the blinding of U.S. eyes in space, so that we would not be able to see what they were up to. Then the Soviets launched their first strike against the United States and Western Europe, using their accurate land-based intercontinental missiles and SS-20s. They followed up with a second strike against U.S. cities, using their less accurate submarine missiles. Then they practiced shooting down the counterattacking U.S. warheads with their antiballistic missiles. All firings were coordinated under a unified Soviet command and control network. The sequence of events was just what would be expected in a surprise attack on the United States and Western Europe. One of the most interesting aspects of this chilling exercise was the key role assigned to killer satellites.

The Soviets also have been working at polishing their techniques for quick fueling and launching of their killer satellites. They have reached the point where they can get a rocket bearing a killer satellite loaded with fuel and ready to launch in 90 minutes. This quick-reaction system permits an attack on an enemy satellite without a lengthy pursuit in orbit. On two occasions, a Soviet killer satellite has also been seen to come up from below and make its kill in a matter of minutes, before it has orbited the earth once.

The quick-kill method confers an important advantage in that it diminishes the chances of the attack being seen from the ground. If one of our satellites suddenly disintegrated in time of peace, we might suspect a Soviet killer satellite, but proving it would be difficult. Several thousand large pieces of debris from previous launches now orbit the earth, as well as many more bits too small to be tracked by radar. Each one hurtles through space at 18,000 miles an hour, faster than an artillery shell. A collision with one of these fragments could disable one of our reconnaissance satellites, and it might be difficult to distinguish such a collision from an attack by a Soviet killer satellite.

One of the peculiar aspects of the Soviet killer satellites is the fact that the Soviet government denies they exist. Soviet spokesmen have described reports about their killer satellites as "the mythical Soviet threat" and "a premeditated lie." When I described the Soviet killer satellites in a televised exchange with a Soviet space scientist over a direct link by communications satellite between Moscow and New York, the

Soviet scientist said flatly that the USSR had never put any weapons in space. But observers in Europe and the United States have seen the killer satellites launched, seen them close in on their targets, and even witnessed the cloud of debris that flies out after the explosion.

A few years ago the United States began to work on its own antisatellite — not a killer satellite, but a rocket-propelled "smart bullet" that goes straight up from the ground and smashes into its target at high speed. The smart bullet, and the rocket that propels it up to satellite altitudes, are mounted under the belly of an F-15 fighter. The F-15 climbs to an altitude of 50,000 feet, pulls up sharply into a near vertical position, and fires the rocket, shooting the bullet upward on a path that intercepts the target satellite in orbit. The rocket cannot aim the bullet accurately enough to produce an actual collision with the satellite, but it does carry the bullet fairly close to its quarry. Once near the target, the smart bullet homes in on it, using a heat-sensitive instrument that can pick out the warm satellite from the cold background of space. The bullet collides with the satellite and destroys it by the force of the impact. The method is what my early mentor, Robert Oppenheimer, would have called a "sweet solution" to a technical problem. However, we are not sure whether it is practical, since it has never been tested against an actual satellite. The Soviet Union tested its killer satellites for years before they worked reliably, and the United States may have to do the same.

The same circumstances that make a satellite a tempting target for destruction by one superpower also make it a valuable asset to the other, and one to be defended at all cost. Fortunately for the side that is trying to protect its satellites in this contest, a satellite can be defended very well. It is sometimes said that satellites are very vulnerable to attack, more so than missiles. However, the reverse is true. A ship cannot be armored too heavily and still stay afloat; a missile cannot be loaded with too much shielding, or it will not get off the ground, but a satellite in orbit is weightless and can be armored as heavily as necessary, within reason, without adverse effects on its performance. A satellite can also be armed with its own weapons, to destroy any intruding satellite that approaches within lethal range. It can shoot down smart bullets with its own smart bullets. And it can be supplied with onboard rocket engines and a large supply of fuel, so that it can maneuver out of the path of an intruder.

Critical satellites can also be protected by placing them in very high orbits, out of the adversary's range. It would take several hours for a killer satellite or a smart bullet to climb 22,000 miles to the altitude of a geosynchronous satellite. That long period gives threatened satellites plenty of time to draw a bead on the approaching killer satellite and destroy it. Or, if the approaching intruder is a smart bullet that seems to be homing in with radar or heat detectors, the satellite under attack can wait until it is quite close and then nimbly step aside. Smart bullets have a limited maneuvering ability; they cannot make a sudden change of course to follow a last-minute change of course by their quarry.

An even greater measure of protection can be obtained by placing key satellites in orbits halfway to the moon, which could take the adversary's killer satellites twelve to twenty hours to reach. Some of the most important battle-management satellites, which would coordinate our defending satellite forces in the event of a massive Soviet missile attack, may be placed in these so-called cislunar orbits.

A satellite could also be protected at any altitude by the methods bomber and fighter pilots use to foil the enemy in aerial combat. If a smart bullet homes in on the satellite with a heat-sensitive instrument, a warm decoy can be tossed out to the side to distract the instrument. If a satellite senses it is being probed by a radar beam — indicating that a killer satellite is stalking it — the satellite under attack can analyze the radar beam and send back spurious pulses that tell the killer satellite, "I'm not here, I'm over there."

Some of these stratagems can also be used by Soviet missiles to evade our defense. Decoy warheads — lightweight imitations of the real warhead — are a particularly useful ploy because we must find a method of discriminating between the decoy and the real warhead, or waste our resources by trying to shoot down everything in sight. However, the number of decoys a missile can deploy is limited by the fact that the missile must rise up against gravity; it cannot carry too much excess baggage in the form of decoys or any other protective device. A satellite, being weightless in orbit, does not have this restriction.

Instruments to detect an adversary's attempts at mischief — the probing radar beam, the laser beam, or the hit scored by a smart bullet — are being installed on U.S. military satellites now under construction, so that in the future we will know when our key satellites have come under attack.

The newest satellite models also are being hardened or protected against the effects of nuclear explosions in space. These explosions generate a pulse of electrical voltage that can burn out radios and hair dryers across a continent and also put a nation's entire satellite fleet out of action. Some defense experts believe that nuclear explosions in space, disabling our satellites by damaging their electronic circuits, will be the first step in a nuclear attack on the United States. However, a thin metal casing around the critical electronic parts can shield the satellite from this effect. Increasing reliance on fiber optics — thin glass wires that replace the electronic circuits in satellites by using pulses of light instead of electricity — can eliminate that problem entirely.

Proliferation is another stratagem available to the defense for the protection of its satellites. This means, for example, putting a silent spare in orbit, which never reveals its presence to the adversary by talking to receiving stations on the ground, but only talks to other American satellites. Hidden in space, the silent spare is instantly available to take over the duties of a satellite that has been hit.

Armor, guns, maneuverability, spoofing, proliferation — these are time-honored methods for protecting valued military assets. They have not been used in space because no one is shooting at today's satellites yet. Tomorrow's satellites will be another story.

6 Missiles

A missile is a tank of fuel with an engine at one end and a bomb at the other. When fuel burns in the engine, hot gases jet out of the exhaust. As the gases leave, they push back on the missile and propel it upward. The strength of the backward push is enormous. In a matter of minutes, it accelerates the rocket to speeds as high as 15,000 miles an hour and altitudes as great as 700 miles.

The working principle of a rocket engine is simpler than that of any other engine. Suppose a chamber or rocket casing is filled with a hot gas and tightly sealed. The gas consists of molecules which continually bombard the walls of the chamber. They move in every direction, and through the impact of these molecules a pressure is exerted on the walls of the chamber. The gas is distributed uniformly through the chamber and therefore the gas molecules hit each wall at the same rate and with the same speed. Accordingly they exert the same forces up and down; and also to the left and to the right. The forces balance, and the casing remains at rest.

Now consider the consequence of removing the bottom wall. The upper force is no longer balanced by the lower one. There is a net force upward, and the rocket takes off.

A continuing supply of hot gas, and a continuing force upward are maintained by burning fuel drawn from the rocket's tank. Large rockets have a rapacious appetite for fuel; the Saturn rocket used for the landings on the moon burned ten tons of fuel each *second*.

The jet engines on a commercial airliner like the 707 work in the same way. Fuel burns in the jet engine, and the hot gases rush out of the engine exhaust and push back on the aircraft, propelling it forward. In fact, commercial airliners and missiles can use the same fuel — kerosene. The main difference between a jet airplane and a rocket is that in the case of the jet, the oxygen needed for burning the fuel comes from the atmosphere where it is present in a rather dilute, gaseous form; whereas a rocket carries its oxygen along with it in a liquid and highly condensed form. Liquid oxygen is about a thousand times denser than the oxygen in the atmosphere. As a consequence of the concentrated supply of oxygen available to the rocket, its fuel burns with ferocious intensity, and generates more energy per pound than the explosion of nitroglycerine. The extraordinarily intense burning creates the enormous forces that boost the rocket to a very high speed in a short time.

The idea of using liquid oxygen in a rocket came from Robert Goddard, an American physics professor. Dr. Goddard tested the first liquid-fueled rocket in 1926 on his "Aunt" Effie's farm in Massachusetts. It rose to a height of 41 feet, traveled 184 feet before it hit the ground, and reached a top speed of 60 miles per hour. Dr. Goddard predicted that man could reach the moon with this invention but very few people believed him. A New York Times editorial rebuked the physics professor for failing to grasp basic principles of science that were "ladled out daily in high schools." After all, said the editorial writer, everyone knew that you couldn't push against a vacuum. But of course Dr. Goddard's science was quite sound, and the *Times* editorial writer was confused.

At any rate, Professor Goddard persisted in his experiments. One day the phone rang, and Charles Lindbergh came on the line. Lindbergh wanted to drive up to Massachusetts to talk to Goddard about his rocket. That evening Professor Goddard told his wife that Lindbergh, the famous aviator had called for an appointment, and she said, ''Yes, and I had tea with Marie, Queen of Rumania.''

Lindbergh was impressed by what he saw. He obtained money for Goddard from the Guggenheim Foundation, and the experiments continued. One rocket rose to a height of 1-½ miles, and another reached a top speed of 500 miles an hour, probably the fastest any man-made device had ever gone up to that time.

The U.S. War Department, informed by Dr. Goddard of his progress, had no quarrel with his basic physics, but found his rockets to be militarily uninteresting. In 1940, with the shadow of war looming over America, Goddard came to Washington to describe his experiments. The officer presiding at the briefing had also heard of work just getting started on the newfangled atom bomb. Getting up at the end of the briefing, he managed to dismiss two of the most significant military inventions in the history of warfare when he said that what we needed in this war was not fancy bombs and rockets, but a better trench mortar.

But in Germany a band of rocket enthusiasts, following along the same path as Dr. Goddard, was received with greater interest by the military leaders of the re-arming German nation. In 1936, the German Army and Air Force jointly kicked in enough money to set up Wernher von Braun and a group of rocket scientists and engineers near the village of Pennemunde. From Pennemunde, a straight line of development led to the V-2 and the bombardment of London in 1945. In all, more than a thousand V-2s were launched against England each carrying a 1500-pound bomb. The V-2s were a terrifying weapon that crossed the Channel in five minutes and descended on their target without noise or other warning. No defense existed against them. However, the Allies overran their launch sites, and the war ended before the V-2 could exact a heavier toll.

The Soviets captured the plans and production facilities for the V-2 and an even larger rocket with twice the range, and scaled them upward to a mammoth rocket designed to carry an A-bomb across intercontinental distances. Then the H-bomb was invented. The H-bomb was considerably smaller and lighter than the A-bomb and did not require a rocket as massive as the scaled-up V-2 the Soviets had built. But a Soviet scientist pointed out that this oversized rocket was powerful enough to put a satellite into orbit. That is how the Russians came to launch the first Sputnik.

Meanwhile, Von Braun and his team had surrendered to the American forces, which brought them to the United States and installed them in the Army arsenal at Huntsville, Alabama. There, Von Braun resumed the line of development that led eventually to the Saturn rocket, project Apollo, and the landing of men on the moon.

Getting back to the immediate post-war period, some American defense experts were still unimpressed by the military potential of the rocket, even with the memory of the V-2 fresh in mind. Dr. Vannevar Bush, who directed the government's science effort during World War II, offered the following wisdom after the war:

> "People who have been writing these things that annoy me have been talking about a 3000-mile rocket shot from one continent to another carrying an atom bomb. . . . I think we can leave that out of our thinking."

However, scientists do not have a good track record at seeing the practical implications in a new invention, and Dr. Bush was no exception. Contrary to his pessimism, the lifting power, range and accuracy of the missile increased steadily, until it became possible to build a missile that would carry the equivalent of a million tons of TNT across thousands of miles of ocean and deposit it on the enemy's doorstep.

This brings us to the present. Missiles today work just the way that Goddard designed them, but they are a great deal bigger. The largest missile in the world, the Soviet SS-18, is taller than a ten-story building, contains 50,000 gallons of fuel and weighs 240 tons. This giant rocket carries a cluster of 10 bombs with a total explosive power of five million tons of TNT — that is more than all the bombs dropped in World War II — on one missile. And the Soviets have hundreds of SS-18s.

The bombs, usually called "warheads," are mounted on a platform known as a "bus" that sits in the nose of the missile. After the missile has burned up its fuel, it separates from the bus and falls back to the earth. The bus, traveling with the momentum the missile has given it, continues upward and onward through space. But now the bus does an extraordinary thing. Under command from a computer in its interior, it swivels about and pushes the warheads into space one after the other, each warhead going in a different direction and with a different velocity. The timing and the push are so carefully timed that every warhead lands within a few hundred yards of its own target. The separate targets were picked out for the warheads before the missile was launched. In this way, a single SS-18 missile can destroy as many as 10 American cities or 10 different military targets.

After the warhead has been pushed off the bus, it continues on its way, arcing through space on its course toward a target in the United States. Generally it reaches a height of about 700 miles above the earth's surface. From this peak altitude it begins to descend, gradually picking up speed under the pull of gravity. As the warhead approaches the ground, and enters the denser layers of the atmosphere, its surface glows red-hot and then white-hot under the heat of friction with the air. A half-inch-thick coating of material protects the warhead from

71

damage during this period of intense heating.

The nuclear explosives in the warhead go off either on reaching the ground, or at some set altitude prior to impact. For soft targets like cities, the explosion occurs in the air. If the target is a military site such as a missile silo or a command bunker, that has been hardened with reinforced concrete, the warhead may be fused to penetrate the ground before exploding. In any event, the nuclear explosive will only detonate if a series of precisely timed electronic steps takes place. Unlike ordinary explosives, nuclear explosives do not go off if you hit them with a hammer or drop them on the ground.

The Soviets have accumulated some 3000 nuclear-tipped missiles with a range sufficient to reach the United States. Some are located on Soviet territory and others on submarines. Nearly all are MIRVed. They carry a total of about 8,500 warheads, each with an average explosive power equivalent to 750,000 tons of TNT. The United States has approximately 2400 land-based and submarine-based missiles with a range sufficient to reach the Soviet Union. They are also MIRVed and carry a total of about 7000 warheads, each with an average explosive power equivalent to 250,000 tons of TNT.

The explosive power residing in the American arsenal works out to half a ton of TNT for every person on the face of the earth. The explosive power in the Soviet arsenal amounts to two tons of TNT for every person on the earth. These enormous arsenals of destruction have been built over several decades because each nation feels its security requires a nuclear arsenal so massive that no power would dare attack it, for fear of the devastating retaliation that would follow. This is the strategy of Mutual Assured Destruction.

The trouble with that Mexican standoff, as President Reagan observed, is that because of the enormous explosive power residing in these terrible weapons, the smallest misstep by either nation can have disastrous consequences for the world. Most people agree that it would be better if we could find another way of protecting ourselves that would permit us to reduce the size of our nuclear arsenal. One way of achieving that aim, if we could make it work, would be to have an actual defense that would shoot down the enemy missiles and warheads as they approach.

How can that be done? How can we destroy an object hurtling through space at a speed of more than 10,000 miles an hour?

The answer is that a missile has two properties that make it extremely vulnerable to destruction. One is the fragility of the missile itself. Missiles have a solid and imposing appearance, but their construction is flimsy. The shell of the SS-18, for example, is made of aluminum no thicker than a shirt cardboard. It does not take much force to rupture this thin metal skin and ignite the thousands of gallons of fuel in the interior. Missiles are thin-walled and fragile because they cannot afford to carry much dead weight. Missiles must sacrifice every possible pound in order to reach the enormous accelerations and speeds that will project their deadly payloads across thousands of miles. If the skin of an SS-18 missile, for example, were made another tenth of an inch thicker, the extra weight of the stronger casing, added up over the entire surface of the huge rocket, would amount to eight tons.* But eight tons is twice the weight of all the warheads on the SS-18. If you tried to strengthen the SS-18 in this way, it would not be able to carry any warheads. From the viewpoint of the Soviets that missile would be useless.

A small, fast-moving projectile could easily puncture the fuel tank of the SS-18 and cause it to explode. Or a laser beam

---

*The extra weight cannot be compensated by decreasing the amount of fuel, because with less fuel the missile will fail to reach its required speed and its warheads will fall short of their targets.

could melt a hole in the skin of the missile with relative ease. If the laser beam only softened the skin, that would probably be enough to destroy the missile, because once the missile's structure is weakened in any way, the entire rocket tends to disintegrate.

The other weak spot in the design of a missile is the computer that guides it on its course. The circuits of this electronic brain can be scrambled by beams of radiation directed at them from great distances, causing the missile to go off course and destroy itself. The bus carrying the warheads is guided by another computer. If the circuits of this computer are scrambled by radiation, the bus will push its warheads off in the wrong directions and at the wrong times, so that they will not reach their targets. And the warhead itself is also controlled by a computer, which times the steps that make its nuclear contents explode. If the circuits in this computer are damaged, the warhead will not blow up, but will bury itself in the ground on impact. The computers and electronic circuits in the missiles and its warheads are a temptation for the scientist trying to find ways of delivering us from the menace of these weapons.

So the paradox of the modern missile is that the very features that make it deadly are also its weak points. The planners of "Star Wars" defense have concentrated on these weak points and have devised special instruments of destruction for each one. The first object of their efforts is the thin metal skin of the missile. Its fragility makes it an attractive target for the laser.

BELIEVES ROCKET CAN REACH MOON

Smithsonian Institution Tells of Prof. Goddard's Invention to Explore Upper Air.

MULTIPLE-CHARGE SYSTEM

Instruments Could Go Up 200 Miles, and Bigger Rocket Might Land on Satellite.

Special to The New York Times.

WASHINGTON, Jan. 11.—Announce-ment was authorized by the Smithsonian Institution tonight that Professor Robert H. Goddard of Clark College had invented and tested a new type of multiple-charge, high efficiency rocket of entirely new design for exploring the unknown regions of the upper air. The claim is made for the rocket that it will not only be possible to send this apparatus to the higher layers of the air, including those beyond the earth's atmosphere, but possibly even as far as the moon itself.

The highest level so far reached with recording instruments is nineteen miles, accomplished with a free balloon. Professor Goddard believes that his new rocket can be sent through the band of atmosphere around the earth, which he says extends some 200 miles out, and that his new rocket will be of great value to the science of meteorology. To send a rocket beyond the earth influence would require an "initial mass" of 1,274 pounds.

The announcement authorized tonight declares that Professor Goddard is at the present time perfecting the reloading mechanism of his rocket, under a grant from the Smithsonian Institution, and

THE FIRST LIQUID-FUELED ROCKET. The liquid-fueled rocket, forerunner of today's missiles, was invented by American physicist Robert Goddard. In 1919 Dr. Goddard published a scholarly treatise on the theory of rockets called *A Method For Reaching Extremely High Altitudes,* in which he mentioned that it might be possible to send a rocket to the moon carrying flash powder to make a visible glow when it hit the moon's surface. This caught the attention of the *New York Times,* which ran a front page story on the moon rocket (*left*).

Goddard successfully launched the first liquid-fueled rocket on March 17, 1926 at his "Aunt" Effie's farm (*right*) in Massachusetts. The rocket climbed 41 feet. Goddard wrote, "It looked almost magical as it rose."

76

THE ROCKET EVOLVES. In 1929, Charles Lindbergh who admired Goddard's work, persuaded Daniel Guggenheim to put up $100,000 for the rocket experiments. Goddard moved out to New Mexico to continue his work with larger rockets *(below)*. Lindbergh flew Harry Guggenheim, Daniel's son, out to New Mexico to visit Goddard and see the rockets *(facing page)*.

One new rocket called "Nell" rose to a height of 2000 feet and reached 500 miles an hour—probably the fastest speed ever achieved by a man-made device. But the rockets often strayed off course. Goddard tackled the problem of making them fly straight by an ingenious method using a gyroscope mounted inside the rocket. When the rocket veered off course, the gyroscope, tending to maintain its original direction, could sense the error and open a valve which forced deflecting plates into the exhaust of the rocket. The deflection of the exhaust forced the rocket back onto the right course.

This method is used in every rocket and missile launched today. Many years later, Wernher von Braun examined Goddard's patents and said, "Dr. Goddard was ahead of us all."

Harry Guggenheim (left), Robert Goddard (center) and Charles Lindbergh, in front of Goddard's launch tower in New Mexico.

THE V-2. When the Germans were raining V-2s on
Britain, they thought they were doing well if a rocket
came within 10 miles of its target. They used to point
their V-2s in the general direction of London and hope
for the best. The sequence of photographs *above*, from

German films, shows a V-2 being launched (1), veering
from its course (2), returning to its launch site (3)
and exploding (4). German leaders found it difficult to
keep the rocket crews at their posts during launches.

7 Lasers

The invention of the laser goes back to a discovery made by Albert Einstein around 1916. Einstein was not trying to invent anything; he was just doing what theoretical physicists like to do — thinking about the nature of the Universe. In this particular case, Einstein was thinking about the nature of light, and about what happens when a beam of light shines through a gas. Some experiments had been done on that subject, and Einstein was trying to explain them.

Einstein found that under some conditions the light in the beam can tickle the atoms in the gas through which it is traveling, so that they emit more light. This discovery seemed very theoretical at the time, but later other scientists realized that it could have an important practical application. They saw that if a beam of light can tickle some atoms to produce more light, then the reinforced beam of light can tickle still more atoms and produce still more light, which tickles more atoms to produce more light, and so on. In other words, a runaway effect develops, that can start with a weak beam and build up to a dazzling intensity.

In order to get this runaway effect to take off, special gases have to be used, and they must be treated in special ways, in a tube with mirrors at each end to reflect the light rays and build up their strength. The device that does all this, and actually produces the intense beam, is called a "laser."*

All this is fairly interesting, at least to a physicist, but seems to have little to do with burning a hole in metal or shooting down a missile. But now we came to a remarkable property of the laser. A beam of light produced by a laser is almost perfectly parallel; every ray in it travels in almost exactly the same direction. This is not true for ordinary light. An ordinary beam of light consists of many different rays (speaking somewhat loosely) all going in somewhat different directions. As a result, the beam widens as it travels through space. The beam from a small searchlight may look like a narrow pencil of light as it crosses your backyard at night. But if you could follow that beam for a mile — assuming it were still visible at that distance — you would find that it had spread out enormously, and was 20 or 30 feet wide.

But the beam of light from a laser is different. If it starts out as a beam the width of a pencil, after it travels a mile it will still be the width of a pencil. In other words, a laser beam does not spread out appreciably as it travels through space. There is some spreading effect, but it is very much less than the spreading of a beam of ordinary light.

What does this have to do with burning holes in a missile? The answer is that when all the separate rays of light in a beam are traveling exactly in parallel, a lens can bring them to a sharp focus at one spot. That makes the focused beam of light very small in diameter, and very intense. Therefore, it is very effective in burning holes through metal and other objects.

*Physicists call the effect Einstein discovered "stimulated emission." LASER stands for Light Amplification by Stimulated Emission of Radiation.

To see the significance of this fact, suppose you focused the light from a 100-watt bulb onto a sheet of paper with a magnifying glass. It would form a bright spot perhaps a quarter of an inch across — intense, but not enough to burn through the paper. But the light from a 100-watt laser, focused by the same magnifying lens, would form a far smaller spot, less than a hundredth of an inch across and a thousand times more intense than the light from the 100-watt bulb. A 100-watt laser beam focused in that way can burn through a piece of steel an eighth of an inch thick. It can drill a clean hole through the hardest of substances, including diamonds and rubies.

Used at a lower power level, the laser beam can assist in delicate eye operations because it can be focused down to a very small diameter. Consider, for example, the condition known as a detached retina*, in which the retina becomes separated from the rear wall of the eye, perhaps as the result of a blow to the eye. A detached retina can cause partial or total blindness. A laser beam a few thousandths of an inch wide, passing freely through the transparent outer part of the eye, can spot weld the detached retina back onto the wall of the eye with tiny, intense pulses of light, each one lasting less than a thousandth of a second. An ordinary beam of light could not be focused into a small enough spot to do that.

When it comes to shooting down missiles with lasers, the same ideas apply as in an operation on the eye, but a laser with more power is needed because the target may be as far away as a thousand miles or more. While laser beams hold together much better than ordinary light beams, they are still not perfect; in the course of traveling as great a distance as a thousand miles, even a laser beam spreads out somewhat. As a consequence, the illuminated "spot" formed on the missile's sur-

---

*The retina, located at the back of the eyeball, is the light-sensitive part of the eye; it is like the film in a camera.

face by the laser beam is no longer a small fraction of an inch in diameter. It is now a few feet across.*

But if the laser beam is diffused across an area two or three feet across, 100 watts will no longer be enough power to melt the metal skin of the missile. It turns out that an ultra-powerful laser, generating many millions of watts, is necessary to melt the missile's skin and do it with the necessary speed, in a few seconds or less. However, lasers that put out more than a million watts have already been tested. Experts in the field see no reason why even bigger lasers cannot be built, to meet the need for the Star Wars defense.

The million-watt laser is not enough. We still need a device — a lens or a mirror — to focus the laser beam accurately on the surface of the missile. If the beam is not focused accurately, the laser defense is in trouble again, because the spot it forms on the missile will not be sufficiently small and therefore sufficiently intense to melt its skin. A lens cannot be used to focus the beam, because the glass in the lens would be melted by the million watts of laser energy passing through it. A concave mirror for reflecting and focusing the laser beam — similar to a shaving mirror, or the mirror in a large astronomical telescope — is better. The laser beam bounces off the mirror instead of penetrating it, and does not heat it as much.

Unfortunately there is still another complication: When the laser beam is reflected by a mirror, some of the light in the beam spills over the edge of the mirror into the surrounding space. This tends to spoil the beam's perfection, because parts of the beam are now traveling at an angle to the beam's main direction. In other words, the beam is no longer perfectly parallel.

The spilling-over effect causes the laser beam to broaden

---

*Of course, a spot a few feet across is still far smaller than the "spot" that would be produced by an ordinary searchlight beam, which would be miles in diameter after the beam had traveled a thousand miles.

slightly as it travels through space. As a consequence, by the time the beam reaches the missile it is less intense, and therefore less effective in melting the missile's skin.

But it turns out that the spilling-over effect depends on the size of the mirror: the larger the mirror the smaller the effect. Calculations show that if the mirror that reflects the laser beam is at least 30 feet in diameter, the beam can be focused to a small enough spot to do its job,* even after it has traveled a thousand miles.

So, the mirror must be very large. It also must be very carefully made, so that the rays of light are focused accurately. If the surface is pitted, or does not have exactly the right shape, some rays of light will be sent askew, and the focus will be blurred. That makes the light less bright, and diminishes the mirror's effectiveness in melting missiles.

The largest mirror used by astronomers in the United States — the mirror in the telescope on Palomar Mountain in California — is only 17 feet across. Building a mirror of that quality, but 30 feet in diameter, could be a very expensive and time-consuming undertaking if Star Wars scientists relied on the old-fashioned methods used by astronomers for building big telescopes. However, new methods have been developed very recently, that make the construction of huge mirrors much cheaper than it was in the past. One technique is to use a diamond cutting tool to cut the mirror down to the right shape quickly, instead of grinding away at its surface to remove a tiny bit of material at a time. Another method, which cuts the cost enormously, is to make a large mirror out of a number of smaller and less expensive mirrors, each one no more than a few feet in diameter. The mosaic of small mirrors is then connected together to function like one mammoth re-

---

*Exactly how big the mirror has to be depends on how powerful the laser is. A 30-foot mirror does the job when combined with a 20-million-volt laser.

flector. These new methods make the cost of building large Star Wars mirrors a thousand percent cheaper than it was in the old days.

One question remains: Where do we put the lasers? They must keep the missile fields of the Soviet Union within their view at all times, which means that they cannot be located in the United States. The best solution to this problem is to locate the lasers in satellites that orbit over the USSR continuously, keeping the Soviet missile fields under constant surveillance.

Finally we have a system that can destroy Soviet missiles at a great distance. It consists of a fleet of satellites orbiting over the USSR, each containing a powerful laser and a large concave mirror, to reflect the laser beam towards the missile and focus it on the missile's skin until the skin softens or melts. The fleet includes enough satellites so that several are over the Soviet Union at all times — a sufficient number to shoot down, in the worst case, all the intercontinental ballistic missiles in the Soviet Union if they are launched against us simultaneously.

8 Other New Technologies

The laser mounted on a satellite is a promising technology for destroying missiles. The neutral particle beam, which shoots a stream of fast-moving hydrogen atoms at the missile, may turn out to be even better. A neutral particle beam, mounted on a satellite, can be lethal to the missile and its warheads in almost any phase of their flight.

The Neutral Particle Beam. This beam of atoms is so effective because it is very penetrating. A laser beam is absorbed at a missile's surface and does not get into the missile's interior, but the atoms in a neutral particle beam pass right through the metal skin of the missile and enter into the brains of the missile — the electronic computer that guides it on its course. There the atoms create spurious pulses of electricity that cause the computer to hallucinate, driving the missile off its proper path so that it begins to tumble and destroys itself. If the beam is intense enough, it can even flip the bits inside the computer's memory so that it remembers the wrong things; or it can cause the computer to lose its memory altogether. Any one of these effects is deadly to the Soviet missile's execution of its task.

The neutral particle beam can also play havoc with the circuits in the computer inside the "bus" that sits on top of the missile and holds the warheads. The mischief created here may prevent the bus from releasing its warheads; or it may cause the bus to send the warheads in the wrong directions, so that they miss their targets; or it may damage the electronic circuits in the warheads themselves, after they have been pushed off the bus, so that when they reach their targets, they fail to explode. All in all, it is a most useful device for anyone trying to shoot down missiles.

The neutral particle beam, like the laser, is based on an ingenious idea. Normally a particle is accelerated to high speeds by applying an electrical force to it. The force acts on the electric charge carried by the particle and makes it move faster. However, the beam of atoms used to destroy missiles does not carry any electrical charge; it is electrically neutral. It *must* be electrically neutral because if it were not — if the atoms carried an electrical charge — the magnetic field of the earth would act on the charge and deflect the path of the beam in an unpredictable way. The beam would wander all over and it would be impossible to aim it so that it struck the Soviet missile or its warheads.

If the atoms in the beam are electrically neutral, the earth's magnetic field does not affect them. But then, by the same token, electrical forces do not affect them either, and it is difficult to accelerate them to high speeds. And if they are not moving at high speeds, they cannot penetrate the skin of the missile and get into its innards to wreck its computers.

In other words, if the beam is electrically charged, it does not travel in a straight line and is useless as a missile killer; and if it is not electrically charged, it cannot be accelerated to high speeds, and is also useless as a missile killer.

The solution to this scientific conundrum has turned out to be simple. Physicists have known for some time that a hydrogen atom, which normally consists of one electron circling around a central nucleus, is capable of holding on to two electrons, although the second electron is held quite weakly. The second electron gives this atom an excess of electrical charge; it is no longer electrically neutral. Therefore, if an electrical force or voltage is applied to the atom, it will pick up speed. After the atom has been accelerated to the desired speed, it is a relatively easy matter to shake loose the extra electron, which, it should be remembered, is not very tightly attached to it. The end result is that we now have a neutral, but fast-moving, beam of atoms.

Improved methods for creating a neutral particle beam were developed by Soviet scientists some years ago, and were discussed extensively in their scientific literature until about ten years ago, when suddenly, all reports on the subject disappeared from view. Apparently the Soviets realized the military applications of what seemed at first to be just another line of basic research. In particular, they may have seen the possibility of using their method to destroy American missiles. At any rate, our scientists picked up the idea from the Soviet reports and set to work to develop the neutral particle beam as a method for destroying missiles. Presumably the Soviets, who invented the method, are also hard at work on developing it as a destroyer of missiles.

The Electromagnetic Railgun. Another new technology, called the electromagnetic railgun, is not itself a destroyer of missiles, but used in combination with smart bullets, it enormously enhances their effectiveness. The trouble with smart bullets as they are used today is that the gun that fires them is a rocket, which only gets the speed of the bullet up to about 10,000 miles an hour. That is no faster than the speed of the Soviet missile the bullet is chasing, which makes it hard for the bullet to intercept its missile. The bullet has to be aimed across the missile's path and considerably ahead of it, anticipating where the missile is going to be several minutes and several thousand miles from now. Predicting the Soviet mis-

91

sile's path that far ahead is difficult. A smart bullet has a limited capability for maneuvering, and if the prediction of the missile's position is not accurate enough to bring the smart bullet fairly close to the target, the bullet's computer brain will not be able to steer it into a collision.

The electromagnetic railgun can get a smart bullet up to much higher speeds than a rocket. In this kind of gun the bullet is mounted on a little sliding carriage between two rails. An electric current of several million amperes flows down one rail and up the other, creating an extremely intense magnetic field between the rails. The magnetic field propels the bullet forward, just as hot gases in a gun barrel propel an ordinary bullet forward. However, the speeds that can be achieved are far greater. Bullets fired from a railgun have already achieved speeds greater than 10,000 miles per hour, the top speed of a missile, and may eventually be able to reach speeds greater than 50,000 miles an hour. At those speeds, they can catch up to and intercept the Soviet missile a thousand miles away in less than a minute.

The main problem with the electromagnetic railgun, as with the laser and the neutral particle beam, is that it is an advanced technology, and working the bugs out of it may take a number of years. As an example of these bugs, railguns accelerate their bullets to high speed very quickly, in about a second. That means an acceleration of thousands of "g's".* The jolt of this explosively rapid acceleration tends to tear the bullet apart and damage its electronic brains. Packing the

*A "g" is the acceleration of an object acted on by gravity. A ball dropped to the ground, for example, picks up speed at the rate of one "g". When a jet takes off and you are pushed back into your seat, you feel an acceleration of one to two "g's". A fighter pilot coming out of a steep dive experiences about ten "g's". Beyond that level, pilots tend to blank out. These numbers will give some feeling for the huge forces created by an acceleration of 50,000 "g's".

brains so they survive the jolt is a serious problem. But progress is being made; recently, engineers succeeded in testing a smart bullet at an acceleration of 50,000 "g's" without addling its electronics. The electromagnetic railgun, used as the propulsion for the smart bullet, may be the first of the new technologies to see service.

The X-ray Laser. The most devastating of the new technologies, and in some respects the most controversial, is the x-ray laser. The details of this device are a tightly kept secret, but it is known that the first step in using it is to explode a nuclear weapon. The laser is mounted next to the nuclear weapon. Of course, the nuclear explosion destroys the laser almost instantly, in less than a millionth of a second, but in the brief interval before the laser is destroyed it produces many beams of very intense x-rays, that can be directed against Soviet missiles and warheads with lethal effect.

Exploding a nuclear weapon does not seem like a very promising start for a defense that is supposed to help rid the world of nuclear weapons. But the nuclear explosion that produces the x-ray laser is exceedingly small compared to the total destructiveness of the weapons it is putting out of action. According to calculations, one x-ray laser the size of a packing crate will be able to destroy the entire Soviet ICBM arsenal — thousands of missiles — if these missiles are launched against us at one time in a massive attack. Furthermore, the explosion that powers the x-ray laser takes place hundreds of miles above the earth, and does not cause damage or radioactive fallout on the ground; whereas the missiles the laser destroys are designed to explode at or near the surface of the earth, with deadly consequences in blast pressure and radioactive poisoning. Nonetheless, the idea of exploding one nuclear weapon to shoot down others — even thousands of others — makes people uneasy. That is one of the reasons the proposal is controversial.

The construction of the x-ray laser has not yet been disclosed, but here is one way it could work. The bomb and the x-ray laser are mounted side by side. When the bomb explodes its temperature quickly rises to many millions of degrees. At this high temperature, the bomb radiates ''heat'' to space in the form of x-rays and gamma rays, which are packets of exceedingly energetic radiation. The x-rays and gamma rays penetrate into the laser, vaporizing it and raising it also to an extremely high temperature. Now the laser is a dense, hot gas of atoms. X-rays and gamma rays from the explosion continue to pour into this gas. The x-rays and gamma rays work their effect on the gas in two steps. First, because the x-rays and gamma rays are so energetic, they knock the outermost electrons on some atoms completely out of their orbits, leaving behind a partially stripped atom. Then, interacting with the stripped atoms, they knock some electrons to higher orbits. An atom with an electron knocked up to a higher orbit is said by physicists to be ''excited.'' An excited atom stays in that condition for a short time — a trillionth of a second or so — and then the electron returns to its normal, lower orbit again. The physicist says the atom has returned to its ''ground state.''

When an excited atom returns to its ground state, it emits a flash of radiation or ''light.'' However, this ''light'' is not the ordinary kind we see by. It is a much more energetic and penetrating kind of radiation; it is, in fact, an x-ray. As soon as a single atom in the gas does this — that is, returns to its ground state and emits a flash of ''light'' in the form of an x-ray, the principle of the laser begins to apply. For an x-ray emitted by one atom can tickle another excited atom nearby, and prompt it to return to its ground state. As the second atom does so, it emits another x-ray. The original x-ray is still there, so that makes two x-rays. Each one of the two can tickle still another excited atom, producing still another x-ray. Now there are four x-rays. The four become eight, the eight become 16, and so on. In a short time a cascade of x-rays develops. At the end, may excited atoms are back in their ground states, no more x-rays can be produced, and the cascade ends. The laser is exhausted.

All this takes place very quickly. The cascade of x-rays builds up, reaches a peak, and declines in less than a billionth of a second.

The result is a brief but incredibly intense burst of x-rays with a power of trillions of watts. That is far more than the total power consumed by the earth's population. This burst of x-rays, directed at a missile, a bus or a warhead, has a shattering effect. The x-ray beam almost instantly vaporizes a thin surface layer of the missile or any other object the beam strikes. The layer of hot vapor explodes outward, kicking back on the material underneath with a force of many tons. The effect on the missile is like hitting it with a sledge hammer, but much worse.

The Excimer Laser. Several other possibilities for destroying missiles are also quite promising. One method uses a special kind of laser called an "excimer" laser. An excimer is a molecule made of two atoms tied together, just as a molecule of oxygen consists of two oxygen molecules bound together. However, the excimer is a very special kind of molecule because its atoms only stay attached to one another when they are in what is called an "excited state" of the molecule. That means some of the electrons have been kicked up to higher orbits.

Once the excimer molecule is formed, it stays in its excited state for a little while (a few billionths of a second), and then the electrons return to their lowest orbits again, and the molecule collapses to what is called its "ground state." However, as soon as the electrons drop back to their ground state, the molecule breaks up into two separate atoms.* Simultaneously, it emits a flash of light which carries away the energy of the excited state.

*The peculiarity of the excimer molecule is that it only stays together when it is in an excited state. When the excimer molecule collapses to the ground state, its two constituent atoms do not attract one another any longer, and the molecule breaks up.

95

With that background, here is how the excimer laser works. The first trick is to produce a very large number of excimer molecules — that is, molecules in an excited state. Unusual combinations of gases have to be used, such as xenon and chlorine, or krypton and flourine. After the excimer molecules are formed, they begin to collapse to their ground state, one after another. Immediately after a molecule collapses to its ground state, it breaks up into two separate atoms. As it collapses, it emits a flash of light.

Now the laser principle begins to apply. Consider the first excimer molecule that decays. It emits a flash of light; that flash of light affects another excimer molecule that has not yet collapsed; by the principle of the laser, the light tickles the other molecule and causes it to collapse also, emitting its own flash of light. The first flash of light is still there, so now there are two flashes of light. Each one tickles still another atom, causing it to collapse and emit still another flash of light. Now there are four. In this way a cascade of light builds rapidly. The cascade of light pours out of the tube containing the excimer molecules as an intense pulse of laser light. When the majority of the excimer molecules have collapsed to their ground states, and separated into atoms, no additional flashes of light can be produced. This terminates the laser action.

In practice, it works out that the beam only lasts for about a millionth of a second before all the excimer molecules are used up. In other words, the beam is a very brief — but very intense — burst of laser light. This intense burst of energy, directed against a missile, can administer a jolt so severe that the missile breaks up.

The Free Electron Laser. Another promising kind of laser for defending against missiles uses a beam of light generated by a stream of fast-moving electrons instead of the atoms of gas that generate the beam of light in other lasers. In this laser, called a free electron laser, a narrow stream of high-speed electrons is sent down a line of magnets. The magnets exert a force on the electrons, bending their paths first one way and then the other, so that the electrons execute a little dance as they go down the line of magnets. At each step in the dance, some electrons emit tiny flashes of light. This is a consequence of a law of physics which states that when an electrically charged particle changes its direction of motion, the particle must emit a flash of radiation.

Now, once again, the principle of the laser applies. Every time an electron emits a little flash of light as it changes direction, the flash of light tends to make neighboring electrons emit additional flashes as they go through their steps in the dance. That is, one flash of light creates conditions for the production of more flashes of light. Those light flashes, in turn stimulate still more flashes. This situation quickly develops into a dazzling cascade of light, that heads out to space as an intense laser beam.

The Electron Beam. Still another way of destroying missiles has come out of a recent discovery at the Livermore Laboratory. The Livermore discovery seems to make the impossible possible, because it provides a method for sending a beam of electrically charged particles in a straight line through the atomsphere. Many physicists thought that could not be done, because the earth's magnetic field exerts a force on electrically charged particles and bends their paths. As a result, a charged particle beam cannot hit anything. Firing a beam of charged particles through the earth's magnetic field is like firing a bullet with a rifle that has a bent barrel. As if that were not enough of a problem, the charged particles in the beam also tend to repel one another, so that the beam spreads apart and swells during its long journey through space. By the time it reaches the target, it may be too dispersed to do any damage.

But the scientists at Livermore have found an ingenious way to get around these problems. Their method starts with a laser. The laser is first used to clear a channel in the earth's magnetic field and then the electron beam that is going to destroy the missile travels through this clear channel. Since there is no appreciable magnetic field in the channel, the electron beam travels in a straight line. Here is how the laser beam clears out the magnetic field. The beam of laser light knocks electrons off some of the atoms of air it encounters on its way to the target. These electrons move in spiraling paths as a result of the force exerted on them by the earth's magnetic field. A law of physics states that the spiraling electrons will generate a magnetic field of their own in the opposite direction to the field that caused them to spiral. That is, they create a magnetic field that tends to cancel the earth's magnetic field. If a beam of fast-moving electrons is now fired down the channel that was created by the laser light, the electrons will move in a straight line because the effect of the laser light has cleared the earth's magnetic field out of the channel.

The method carries a bonus. Some of the electrons that were knocked out by the laser beam have such high velocities that they leave the channel entirely. Since electrons are negatively charged, when a number of electrons depart from the channel, a net residue of positive electric charges is left behind. Now, when the beam of electrons is fired down the channel towards the target, the positive electric charge in the channel tends to hold on to the negatively charged electrons, and keeps them from dispersing. In other words, it tends to hold the electron beam together, so that when the beam strikes the target it hits it with greater energy.

It seems that scientists designing a defense against missiles may some day have an embarrassment of riches to choose from. The potential of the new technologies will not be clear for another three to five years, and some years beyond that may be needed to shape the best of them into practical defenses against missiles, which means that these new technologies may not come into use before the mid or late

1990s. But long before any of the new devices becomes available as a weapon, it should be possible to build an effective defense against missiles with the off-the-shelf, mature and unexotic technology of the smart bullet propelled by an ordinary rocket.

9 Protection for the 1990s

An advanced defense against Soviet missiles, using exotic technologies such as the laser and the neutral particle beam, may become a reality by the end of the century. Americans will rest easier when that defense is in place, for it will mean that the prospect of a Soviet first strike is essentially nil.

Meanwhile, the technologies that are already in hand will allow us to put into place in the early 1990s, a simple but highly effective defense at a cost of roughly $60 billion. A conservative estimate of the effectiveness of this defense is 90 percent, which means that only one Soviet warhead in ten will reach its target. This is more than sufficient to guarantee devastating U.S. retaliation and discourage Soviet leaders from any thought of achieving a successful strike.

This limited defense will be based on the off-the-shelf technology of the smart bullet. That technology is mature and unexotic and its deployment around the end of the decade involves no further research, but only a relatively modest degree of engineering development of existing hardware. In fact, it is technically accurate to state that these vital defenses could be in place at this moment if it were not for the constraints accepted by the United States in its adherence to the ABM treaty.

The defense will consist of two layers — a boost-phase defense that tackles the Soviet missiles as they rise above the atmosphere, and a terminal defense that intercepts the warheads at the end of their trajectories, as they descend toward their targets in the United States.

The boost-phase defense will necessarily be based in space because it depends on satellites for the surveillance of the Soviet missile fields and the tracking of the missiles as they rise from their silos. The satellites are also needed to store the smart bullets that will be fired at the Soviet missiles early in their flight. All these operations can only be carried out from space platforms orbiting over the Soviet Union.

Of the two layers in the defense, the boost phase is by far the more important. A boost-phase defense is essential because it prevents the Soviets from concentrating their warheads on high-priority targets such as our own missile silos or the Trident submarine bases. The Soviets cannot do this if we have a boost-phase defense, because they cannot tell beforehand which booster, and which warheads, will get through and which ones will be destroyed.

This fact is so important that it warrants a fuller discussion. It is often stated that a simple ground-based defense of our missile silos — that is, guns or rockets that fire smart bullets, located right next to each cluster of silos — would be sufficient to restore the credibility of our land-based deterrent. It is particularly necessary to protect the silos containing our Minuteman III ICBM's. These are the only missiles in the possession of the United States with the combination of yield and accuracy required to destroy hardened Soviet military sites and the 1,500 hardened bunkers that would shelter the Soviet leadership. But their very importance to us illustrates

101

the difficulty of a point defense, because the value of the silos to us means they will be among the highest-priority targets in any Soviet first strike. The Russians can overwhelm any point defense we place around those silos, if they wish to do so, by allocating large numbers of warheads to these critical targets. If our defense includes a boost-phase defense, that becomes enormously more difficult for them.

The boost-phase defense is very important for another reason. It is more effective in dealing with the menace of the Soviet SS-18 missiles. These are monster missiles, each twice as large as an MX. They carry 10 warheads each, but probably can be loaded with 20 to 30 warheads each, depending on yield, if the Soviets judge this to be in their interest. That means the Soviets could add thousands of ICBM warheads to their arsenal at relatively modest cost. With numbers like that, the ratio of costs of offense over defense might tilt in the Soviet favor if we had a terminal defense alone. But a boost-phase defense, which destroys a missile near the beginning of its flight, eliminates all 20 to 30 warheads at one time. It solves the SS-18 problem.

The only technology available for an early 1990s boost-phase defense is the "smart bullet" — a projectile that homes in on its target using radar or heat waves, and destroys it on impact. That technology is available today; the boost-phase defense need not wait for the availability of the more devastating technologies of the laser, the neutral particle beam or the electromagnetic rail gun. The interceptor rocket for this early boost-phase defense would be an advanced version of the air defense interceptors that are in operational use in the Air Force today. The boost-phase interceptor rockets would weigh about 500 pounds; the interceptors themselves — the smart bullets — weigh 10 pounds; they are nonnuclear; and their speed is about 4 miles per second. The F-15-launched ASAT is another technology that could also be adapted to a boost-phase defense against missiles.

The rockets with their smart bullets would be stored in pods on satellites and fired from space. The tracking information needed to guide them would be acquired from satellites orbiting over the Soviet missile fields.

Satellites in high, geosynchronous orbits 23,000 miles up, hover over the Eurasian land mass and scan the Soviet missile fields continuously for signs of an attack. Heat-sensitive "eyes" on the satellites look for the telltale flames of the missile launch, follow the course of the missile as it rises, and pass their information on to computers which calculate the probable path of the missile over the oceans or the north pole.

Within seconds, the computers provide a picture of the entire attack: How many missiles are there? What kind? Headed toward which targets in the United States? The high-altitude satellites flash their information to the fleet of satellites at lower altitudes — the battle management satellites and the satellites that carry the weapons to be used against the Soviet missiles. These satellites begin to track the moving missiles. In a matter of a few more seconds, they fire. The boost-phase defense has begun.

Satellites are critical throughout this operation. It is not possible to build an effective defense against Soviet missiles without using satellite platforms orbiting over the USSR. Efforts by the Soviet Union and by some domestic critics of strategic defense to knock out the so-called "space weapons" aspect of strategic defense are tantamount to eliminating the boost-phase defense and would destroy the effectiveness of the system.

One of the pacing items in this 1990s defense is the computer hardware and software needed to make our satellites reliable and intelligent. Reacting quickly to the attack, tracking the Soviet missiles and warheads, aiming our guns, keeping the master file on thousands of warheads and decoys, shifting our forces from one region to another with the vicissitudes of battle — all these tasks carried out simultaneously will require several billion operations, or basic units of arithmetic and thought, per second. The newest computers are already close to this capability and computing speed is not expected to be a major problem for our defense.

Of course, that would not have been true as recently as 10 years ago. As has been widely remarked, the increases in the speed of computers has been phenomenal in the last decade. This is one of the reasons why a defense against Soviet missiles is possible today but was not possible in the recent past.

The preparation of the complex computing programs needed is another matter. This is one of the long poles in the program, and is receiving a great deal of attention in early planning. Error-free operation is essential, for a single mistake could be fatal to the survival of the United States in this battle. But how can this impossible goal be achieved? The designers of the defense system plan to use the same method nature employs to get around the effects of serious errors in the human brain. Our brains function without substantial impairment, even if a slice of cerebral cortex is destroyed as a result of an accident, because the wiring in the brain includes heavily redundant circuits and programs that carry out the thought processes and calculations many times along parallel paths. In the same way, computers that direct our space-based defenses will continue to function even if some electronic circuits are damaged, or go out of order, or make a mistake.

The cost of an early 1990s, space-based boost-phase defense of this kind is about $45 billion. That ballpark figure includes 100 satellites, each holding 150 interceptors — sufficient to counter a mass Soviet attack from all 1400 silos; plus 4 "early-warning" satellites in geosynchronous orbits, and 10 lower-altitude satellites dedicated to surveillance, acquisition, tracking and kill assessment; plus the cost of the facilties for ground control communications and battle management.

After the booster has burned out and fallen away and the

warheads arc up and over through space on their way to the United States, the second layer of the defense, called the terminal defense, comes into play. Interception of each warhead will occur as it descends to the earth near the end of its flight. If possible the interception will be at a considerable altitude, well above the atmosphere, to provide a "wide area" protection for the terrain below.

However, interception above the atmosphere makes the discrimination between real warheads and the dummy warheads or "decoys" more difficult. The reason is that the decoys are always lighter than the real warheads, and therefore held back more by air resistance as they enter the atmosphere. So they can be told apart easily. But outside the atmosphere, in the vacuum of space, everything "falls" at the same rate. Separating the decoys from the real warheads requires new instruments and techniques that still require development. If these techniques are not available for deployment in the early 1990s, the interception will take place lower down in the atmosphere. Even so, destruction of the warheads will take place at a sufficiently high altitude, above 100,000 feet, so that there is no ground damage from warheads fused to explode on approach of the intercepting bullet.

The technology used for a terminal defense above the atmosphere could be a small homing interceptor, also, nonnuclear, with a heat-seeking sensor, launched by a rocket weighing one to two tons at a cost of a few million dollars each. This is today's technology, and the interceptors can be available for deployment in five years if a decision is reached to follow that course. One concept for this technology was tested successfully last June by the Defense Department, when an intercepting missile zeroed in on an oncoming warhead at an altitude of 100 miles and totally destroyed it. The technology for a terminal defense within the atmosphere would be somewhat different, but would probably also depend on heat-seeking missiles.

105

The cost of this terminal layer of the defense will be $15 billion. This includes $10 billion for 5000 interceptors at $2 million each, plus $5 billion for 10 aircraft carrying instruments for acquisition and tracking of the warheads, at $500 million each.

The total cost of the two-layer defense as described is $60 billion. This cost estimate is preliminary but believed to be good to 50 percent. Even with its uncertainty, it is certainly an affordable outlay for the protection of the American people from a nuclear first strike. In fact, compared with the outlays projected in the same period for the strengthening of our defense by the modernization of U.S. strategic offensive forces, this limited strategic defense is highly cost-effective. For, as our defenses go into place incrementally, we can gradually build down our offensive forces. That is the expressed hope of the Reagan administration, and the basis of our negotiating position in Geneva. Because of the new technologies, this hope can become a reality.

SMART ROCKS. The facing page shows a cutaway model of a "smart rock" or "smart bullet"—the most fully developed technology for destroying missiles and warheads. It is 10 inches long and weighs about 15 pounds.

The diagram *(below)* shows how this "smart" projectile works. Heat rays from the target, indicated by dashed lines, enter the front end of the projectile, are reflected from the large mirror (1) to the small mirror (2) and then back to the heat-sensitive detector (3). Analyzing the position of the spot of heat on the detector, the projectile's computer (4) calculates the direction to the target. The computer now issues instructions in two steps. First, it directs tiny rockets on the rim of the projectile to fire in such a way as to change the projectile's orientation in space. When the right orientation is achieved, the computer issues a command to the main rocket (5) to fire, shifting the path of the projectile by the amount needed to put it on a collision course.

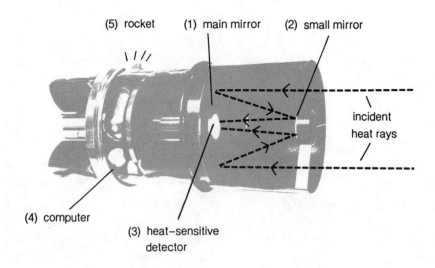

THE COLLISION. High speed collisions can yield considerably more energy per pound than a TNT explosion. The aluminum block *(right)* was hit by a ⅓-ounce projectile traveling at 15,000 miles an hour—typical speed for a collision with a warhead. The plastic object at the center indicates the size and shape of the high-speed projectile. The ruler shows that the collision blasted a 4-inch deep pit in the block.

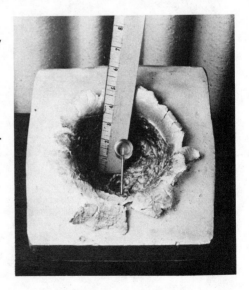

109

DESTRUCTION OF A WARHEAD
The photograph *(left)* shows the rocket used to destroy a warhead at an altitude of more than 100 miles, in a test of terminal defense on June 10, 1984.

The rocket carried a small heat-seeking missile which detected the relatively high temperature of the oncoming warhead against the cold background of space. The rocket was deliberately mis-aimed by 20 miles to test the capability of the interceptor. The interceptor recognized and corrected for the large miss distance and zeroed in for a bull's-eye collision.

Immediately before impact the heat-seeking projectile unfurled a 15-foot metal net *(below)*, resembling
the frame of an umbrella, and studded with steel
weights. The relative speed of the collision with the
warhead was more than 10,000 miles per hour.

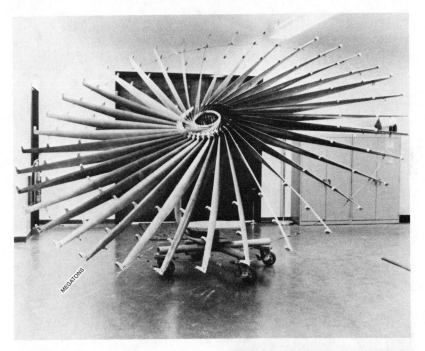

The impact "vaporized" the
warhead and the intercepting
projectile, spreading debris over
an 80-mile area. The photograph *(right)* shows the cloud of
debris, estimated to contain
about a million fragments.

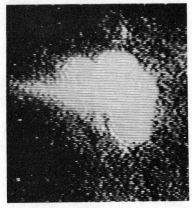

10 The Battle

Much of the discussion of the Star Wars defense assumes a layered defense with four or more distinct layers. In the first layer our defense attacks the Soviet missiles as they rise above their silos. The second layer attacks the warheads that have gotten through the first layer, as they arc through space on their way to the United States. The third layer attacks the warheads that have gotten through the second layer, as they descend to the earth again. And so on.

The idea behind having several layers is that the whole defense can be made nearly perfect in this way, even if the individual layers are less than perfect. Suppose, for example, that the defense has four layers and each layer by itself has an effectiveness of 80 percent. That is, four out of five missiles or warheads entering a layer, get shot down before they leave it, and one in five get through. Then the combined effectiveness of the four layers is 99.8 percent.* That means that only two

---

*This can be seen in the following way. Twenty percent of the warheads get through the first layer; 20 percent of that fraction, or a net of 4 percent, get through the second layer; 20 percent of that 4 percent, or 0.8 percent, get through the third layer: and finally 20 percent of that 0.8 percent, or a net of 0.2 percent, get through the fourth layer.

Soviet warheads out of every 1000 reach their target.

The first layer of the defense goes into effect as soon as the Soviet missiles, also known as "boosters," are launched. This layer is called the boost-phase defense. The boost-phase defense offers the greatest payoff to the defender because at this early stage the missile has not yet sent any of its warheads on their separate paths. Since the largest Soviet missiles carry at least 10 warheads each, if our defense can destroy one of these missiles at the beginning of its flight, it will eliminate 10 or more warheads at a time.

The missile usually burns for three to five minutes. During that time the flame of its exhaust is very conspicuous and can be picked up easily by heat-sensitive detectors. We have three "early warning" satellites in high orbits, with heat-sensitive detectors designed just for this purpose. These satellites detect any missile launched in the Soviet Union, or in any other part of the world, and send an alert within seconds to our NORAD command post, buried under a mountain in Colorado, and to the Pentagon, telling how many missiles have been launched and the targets in the United States they are headed for. If an attack seems to be underway, a message goes to the President and the military commanders. The President decides whether to launch a counterattack, and passes the instructions for firing our missiles down the chain of command, if he deems that response necessary.

When we have a defense in place over the Soviet Union, the early warning satellites will still be our first line of defense, alerting U.S. authorities to any Soviet attack, as before. However, we will also have satellites orbiting at lower altitudes, which will manage the battle that now ensues as our defensive forces swing into action.

The battle management satellites house powerful computers and sensitive instruments that study the attacking Soviet missiles. The satellites pass their information around from one to the other, and pool it to form a coherent picture of the entire attack. Then they assess the disposition of our defending forces — that is, the satellites that will shoot down the missiles — to find out which satellites are over the Soviet missile fields and in a good position to start shooting; which ones are on the fringe of the battle and just moving into position; and which satellites are too far away to play any role in the battle at all.

After that, the battle management computers assign targets to each weapons-carrying satellite according to a prearranged battle plan. One way of doing this is to have a satellite pick out the missile closest to it and go after that first; and then to turn to the one that is next closest and take it out; and so on. But it may not be desirable for the weapons-carrying satellites to pick their own targets. This is one of the prime areas for research. Should the weapons satellites act on their own, or take their orders from the battle management satellites? If the weapons satellites are autonomous, with their own tracking and aiming instruments, they can function even if contact is lost with the commanders — the battle management satellites — like a machine-gunner cut off from his unit.

On the other hand, the battle management satellites, looking down over the entire battle, can make more intelligent decisions about the deployment of our forces for maximum effect. For example, suppose the motions of our weapons-carrying satellites in their orbits just happen to bring several together over one area of the Soviet Union, while another area is bare of satellites. This means a hole has opened up in our defensive screen, through which many Soviet missiles can escape. The battle management computers, orbiting high over the battle, will take note of this situation and instruct some of the more distant weapons satellites to plug the hole by swinging their laser beams around and covering the undefended area. Or they can hurl into the fray other satellites just coming over the horizon, that are on the fringe of the battle.

The weapons satellite is like the soldier in the field; as the smoke and confusion of the battle swirl around him, he cannot see the larger picture. The battle management satellite is the general, overseeing the operation and moving his forces about.

The attention of the battle management satellites and the weapons satellites is concentrated on the boosters as long as they are burning. When the boosters have burned out, the first stage of the battle is over. The boosters release their payloads — the buses carrying the warheads — and fall away. They are no longer of interest. The battle management satellites and the weapons satellites begin to examine the buses, with a view to destroying them. The second stage of the defense, called the post-boost-phase, defense begins.

The buses, each powered by its own small rocket, continue on through space after they separate from the boosters. The buses now go through a little dance in which they pirouette with the aid of their rockets and push off their warheads one by one, each in a different direction, so as to reach a different target in the United States. All this is part of the predetermined Soviet plan for the attack. The steps in the dance that release the warheads are programmed into the bus's computer. This is why an attack that damages or confuses the computer is just as good for our defense as blowing up the entire bus.

It takes the bus several minutes to get rid of all its warheads. During that time it is a very attractive target. If we can destroy the bus, or confuse its computers near the beginning of its dance, we neutralize all the warheads it has on board in one blow. This is as good as destroying the missile would have been. If we catch the bus later, while it is still in the middle of its task of dispensing warheads, we still get several warheads with one hit. All in all, the post-boost-phase defense is almost as useful to us as the boost-phase defense was. It gives us another chance to catch the Soviet missile with all its eggs in one basket, so to speak. And it lengthens by several minutes the time available for accomplishing that task.

As soon as the bus pushes off all its warheads, it is no longer of interest to us. The post-boost-phase of the defense has ended. The defense now turns its attention to the warheads that escaped the first two layers of the defense and are on their way to the United States. This marks the beginning of the third, or mid-course, layer in the defense, in which we try to destroy the separate warheads.

But now the problem becomes considerably more complicated for our defense, because each bus is certain to carry, in addition to its real warheads, a large number of lightweight decoys that are released at the same time as the warheads. The decoys look like warheads in almost every respect but they have no nuclear explosives inside. Their purpose is to confuse our defenses and allow the real warheads to slip through unscathed.

There may be ten decoys for every warhead, thousands or tens of thousands of decoys in all. The flock of warheads and decoys coursing through space in a compact cluster, is called the "threat cloud." How do we see through its disguise to pick out the warheads?

Defense experts have figured out the solution. A decoy is necessarily thin and flimsy in its construction; if it were sturdily built, it would weigh nearly as much as a warhead, and in that case the Soviets might as well put a bomb inside and have the use of the real thing. Being flimsily made, the decoy tends to lose its heat quickly as it flies through the cold of space. The true warhead, which is solidly built, will retain its heat longer. If our satellites carry sensitive infrared detectors — that is, instruments to pick up faint emanations of heat — they can observe the flocks of decoys and warheads and notice which ones are cold, and which ones are relatively warm. The cold objects must be the decoys and the warm ones must be the real warheads.

Soviet technicians could try to foil this method by installing small gadgets inside the decoys to release heat at a controlled rate, so that the decoys are as warm as the warheads. However, this must be done carefully to fool us. Not only must the temperature of the decoy be about the same as the temperature of the real warhead, but it must also change at the same rate, as both fly through space. Otherwise our own instruments and computers will notice the discrepancy and see through the Soviet trick. Now, controlling the heat source inside the decoy so that its temperature changes in a special way is not difficult, but it does require electronic circuits and a simple computer. The weight of the electronics, added to the weight of the heat source, begins to make the decoys heavy. If the decoys are heavy, there is no room for a large number of them in the buses, and they are less useful as a Soviet ploy.

Another way to tell the decoys from the warheads is to tap both with a weak pulse of laser energy and then observe how they recoil. The decoys, being light in weight, will recoil from the tap more rapidly than the heavy warheads. Once the decoys are identified in this way, we can ignore them and attack the true warheads with smart bullets and other weapons. Still another method for solving the decoy problem is to direct a moderately intense burst of laser energy at everything. The laser heat will burn up the thin-walled, fragile decoys, leaving the sturdy warheads undamaged. Then we go after those with our heavy guns.

Of course, the Soviets can always make their decoys robust enough to survive a laser attack. And they can design the insides of the decoys so elaborately that they are able to fool every kind of instrument in our defense. But then the decoys will have so much electronics and special equipment packed into them, that they will weigh nearly as much as the warheads. Once again, if a decoy weighs as much as a warhead the Soviets cannot release a flock of them, and they are of little value.

Throughout the long mid-course flight of the warheads —

lasting about twenty minutes, longer than any other stage — instruments mounted on our satellites will be taking a jaundiced look at the Soviet warheads and decoys. The satellites will be forming images of them in different kinds of light, tapping them with lasers, and steadily acquiring more information about their weight, size, appearance and temperature. The initial stage in the examination will be conducted by the same satellites that supervised the boost-phase defense. The boost-phase satellites will set up a file on each object in the Soviet threat cloud. Later, as the warheads and decoys pass out of range of the boost-phase defense, these will hand over their files to another set of satellites, which will follow the swarm of objects all the way to the United States.

The two sets of satellites talk to each other constantly and pool their observations in a master file that provides birth to death tracking on every potential threat coming our way from the Soviet land mass. As soon as a decoy is identified, or a warhead is destroyed, its file is closed. At the start of the midcourse stage, this master file may contain entries for hundreds of thousands of objects — warheads, decoys, pieces of destroyed bus or warhead, and other debris — but toward the end, as a result of attrition, only a few hundred potentially threatening objects may remain.

Destruction of this remnant of the original threat cloud is the objective in the fourth and final stage of the defense — the terminal defense, which goes into action as the warheads descend toward the earth and approach their targets.

In the terminal defense, the Soviet warheads are close enough to U.S. soil so that satellites are unnecessary. The terminal defense is the only layer of our defense that will be ground-based on U.S. soil, as are the computers that update the master files on approaching objects. Interception of the warheads will take place in space over the United States or near its borders. The interception will be at high altitudes, to protect the ground beneath from the impact of an explosion in case the Soviets wire their warheads to explode automatically on approach of an intruder. As long as the nuclear explosion happens above 50,000 feet, its effects will not be very damaging at ground level, either in radioactive fallout or in blast damage. Progress in developing the weapons for the terminal defense indicates that making the kill at altitudes above 50,000 feet is not an especially difficult task.

The weapons employed in this terminal stage are almost certain to be smart bullets. Rockets launched from American soil carry the smart bullets to within a few miles of the rapidly moving warheads. When the bullets are that close, their instruments and computers take over and maneuver them into a collision course for the kill.

Part III: Strategic and Political Dimensions

11 The Soviet Response

The Soviet government reacted very sharply to President Reagan's plan for a defense of the United States against Soviet missiles. Soviet President Andropov called the proposal "insane" and said it was "a bid to disarm the USSR." According to Soviet officials, if America built a defense against Soviet nuclear attacks, the United States might then attack the USSR with impunity, knowing that it would be protected against Soviet retaliation. In other words, an American defense against Soviet missiles would be threatening to the Soviet Union because it would give the United States a first-strike capability. The Union of Concerned Scientists said the Soviets might even feel so threatened by this possibility that they would preempt — that is, they would attack us before we did anything, just to keep us from building the defense.

But this line of thinking rests on an assumption. The assumption is that the United States would have a defense against Soviet missiles, but the Soviets would not have any corresponding defense against American missiles. But the assumption is false, because the Soviets are working as hard as they can on their own missile defense program, and have been for more than a decade. If one country gets a missile defense before the other, it will be the Soviet Union that does so and not the United States.

As a point of fact, the Soviet Union has been testing its defenses against American missiles ever since it signed the ABM treaty. In 1973, the Soviets began to test their surface-to-air missiles at altitudes close to 100,000 feet. Fifty to sixty tests of this kind were carried out between 1973 and 1975. Surface-to-air missiles are supposed to be used for defense against aircraft, but aircraft do not travel at an altitude of 100,000 feet. However, missiles do. The Soviets were testing their air-defense missiles in what is called an "ABM mode." Such tests are specifically outlawed by the ABM treaty.

The first Soviet ABM tests used a surface-to-air missile called the SA-5, which is not very powerful. A few years ago the Soviet Union began to test a better surface-to-air missile, the SA-12, which can accelerate to the speed of an ICBM — about 12,000 miles an hour — from a standing start in a matter of seconds. The SA-12, used as an anti-ballistic missile, is a serious threat to the security of the United States because it is fast enough to shoot down our submarine-based missiles, which are the mainstay of the American nuclear deterrent.

Recently, evidence came to light of another Soviet violation of the ABM treaty. The new evidence was provided by Big Bird, a reconnaissance satellite. Big Bird discovered a radar of a special type called "phased-array," deep in the interior of the Soviet Union, near the village of Abalakova in south-central Siberia.* A phased-array radar, which consists of thousands of little radars connected so that they sweep the sky electronically, is a major improvement over the rotating radars which can be seen at airports. This kind of radar is par-

*The location of the radar is sometimes identified by the nearby city of Krasnoyarsk.

ticularly useful in shooting down enemy missiles because it can create a highly detailed and accurate picture of a missile attack. One phased-array radar, backed up by a large computer, can keep track of hundreds of separate attacking missiles, figure out their paths, and assign defending missiles to intercept and destroy them.

Phased-array radars are also useful in providing warning of a missile attack. We have several of these so-called "early-warning" radars on the East and West Coasts of the United States. To be useful in giving warning of a missile attack, a radar must be located where it can pick up reflections from the attacking missile at the earliest possible moment. In other words, it has to be placed on a country's borders. The ABM treaty, recognizing this fact, says that each country is permitted to have large phased-array radars provided they are located "along the periphery of its national territory and oriented outward," and are therefore usable for early warning. However, the treaty forbids locating such radars in the interior of the U.S. or the USSR.

That is why American officials are upset about the phased-array radar at Abalakova. It is located in the middle of the Soviet Union, 600 miles from the nearest border. Furthermore, it is not oriented outward toward the border. Instead, it faces toward the Bering Sea and Alaska, about 2000 miles away. Soviet officials say it is designed for tracking satellites, but it has every characteristic of a radar intended for defending the USSR against American missiles. In fact, it is ideally located for tracking missiles launched from American submarines in the Bering Sea off the Soviet coast. The Abalakova radar is just the kind of radar that is outlawed by the ABM treaty.

The essence of the matter is that the Soviet Union has already assembled many of the pieces necessary for a nationwide defense against American missiles. The Soviets can put those pieces together at any time, and on short notice. They have their own unexotic, off-the-shelf technology already deployed — it is called the Galosh antiballistic missile, and large numbers are set up around Moscow. This is the world's only operational ballistic missile defense system. Furthermore, Soviet research on lasers and other advanced Star Wars technologies is going full blast. Dr. James C. Fletcher, former head of NASA, who directed a study of missile defense and examined intelligence reports on the Soviet program, says there is "striking evidence that the Soviet Union has pursued with vigor all the [missile defense] technologies we have recommended and many which we do not even understand yet." Against the background of this vigorous Soviet "Star Wars" activity, complaints by Soviet leaders about our own Star Wars research seem to be lacking in substance.

Some American scientists say that while it may be true that the Soviets are working on a missile defense system, they are going at the matter slowly and not very effectively. According to these scientists, if the United States proceeds with its research on missile defenses, the Soviet scientists will be driven to intensify their efforts. Then they will come up with a much better system than they would have developed otherwise. In other words, the American program will start a "defensive arms race" in space. But intelligence reports available to Dr. Fletcher indicate that we could not start an arms race with our Star Wars program, because the Soviets are already racing. According to Dr. Fletcher, "The Soviet Union is pursuing their [Star Wars] program at the fastest pace their technology allows. It is unlikely that they could accelerate their effort more than they have, *whatever we do.*"

Apparently the pace of the Soviet "Star Wars" program is driven by internal Soviet decisions about what is needed for their security. No "action-reaction" phenomenon is at work here. This is not only so for the unexotic technologies like the Galosh or the smart bullet, but also for the lasers and other exotic defenses. Dr. Fletcher reports that the Soviets are "pursuing with undeniable vigor research on directed energy weapons [i.e., lasers and particle beams]."

The evidence for a substantial Soviet "Star Wars" program is at variance with the beliefs of many American scientists, who tend to discuss "Star Wars" as if the decision to go ahead with it rests with the United States alone. The situation is reminiscent of the controversy over the H-bomb in the early 1950s. Confident in the superiority of American research, our scientists and politicians were certain at that time that the decision to build this weapon rested solely with us. But we now know that the Soviets were hard at work on their own version of the H-bomb as we argued over whether it would be built at all.

Today, as we again debate the wisdom of research in another military area — this time, an area in which the destruction of other weapons is the objective, rather than the destruction of cities and people — we assume that the decision about whether this is done at all will be made in our country, whereas, in fact, the Soviet Union has been hard at work on its "Star Wars" program for several years, and has spent more on its defenses against missiles than it has on its massive offensive arsenal.

But if the Soviets are already working on their "Star Wars" defense as hard as they can, and could not possibly accelerate that effort, what other options are open to them for countering our program? Soviet leaders have frequently given their answer. If the United States puts up a shield against Soviet missiles, then, as a Soviet spokesman said, the Soviet Union "will do its best to get a sharper and heavier sword." In other words, the USSR will build more missiles in an effort to overwhelm our defense. The result will be an acceleration of the arms race and more nuclear weapons in the world.

But some thought and calculation indicate that this Soviet threat is empty. Suppose the United States puts up a two-layer defense using smart bullets. And suppose that this defense can shoot down — as an extremely conservative estimate — 80 percent, or four-fifths, of the Soviet missiles and warheads in a mass attack. That defense is not a nebulous possiblity; it depends on technologies that already exist, and it could be in place today if we had started to work on it five years ago. Suppose now that the Soviet decided they wanted to build enough missiles and warheads so that the number getting through our two-layer defense would be the same as the number that would have reached the United States if we had no defense. This is what "overwhelming the defense" means. Now, the Soviets have 1400 missile silos and missiles that could be launched in a nuclear first strike against the United States. To overwhelm our defense, they would have to launch five times as many as they now have, or 7000 missiles.

But to get their arsenal of missiles up to 7000, the Soviet Union will have to build an additional 5600 missiles. The USSR spent approximately half a trillion dollars in the last 20 years on building the 1400 land-based missiles it now has. To add 5600 more missiles — four times as many — to its arsenal would cost it 4 × $500 billion or $2 trillion more. The Soviet Union would be very hard pressed to spend another $2 trillion on missiles in the next five or six years, on top of its present military outlays.

Two trillion dollars, give or take some hundreds of billions, would be the cost to the Soviet government if it decided to try to overwhelm an 80-percent-effective defense with one lump-sum expenditure. But some experts prefer to look at the matter in another way. They ask "What is the ratio of *marginal* costs? For each extra dollar we spend on our defense, how many dollars will the Soviet Union have to spend on countering that dollar's worth." The point here is that if we put our defenses in place incrementally, and it costs the Soviets less money to counter each addition to our defense than it cost us to build that addition, they win; they can outbuild us. But if their "marginal cost" is greater — if it costs them, say, $2 to

counter our defense for every dollar we spend on making that
defense better, then we win, because if they try to outbuild us,
they will go bankrupt before we do.

This question of marginal cost, or cost ratios, has been
looked at by experts in the Department of Defense and scientists at Los Alamos and Livermore. The Los Alamos team
found that for the kind of defense envisaged as the second
layer of our two-layer smart-bullet defense — that is, the
defense that intercepts Soviet warheads in the final stages of
their flight as they descend towards their targets — the ratio of
costs favors our defense over their offense by at least three to
one. In other words, if the Soviets want to overwhelm our
defense, they must spend three dollars on adding missiles and
warheads, for every dollar we spend on making our defense
better. With a ratio like that, they would find it exceedingly
costly to accelerate the arms race by building more missiles,
as they have threatened to do.

What about the marginal costs for the first layer of the
defense — the so-called space-based or satellite layer? If this
space-based defense is of the off-the-shelf variety, using smart
bullets, the satellites in the American defensive screen will
cost approximately half a billion dollars each. One of these
satellites can destroy 14 Soviet SS-18 missiles. The Soviet
missiles cost about $100 million each, or $1.4 billion for 14.
Comparing this to the cost of our satellite, the ratio of costs
favors the American defense over the Soviet offense by about
three to one — the same as the ratio of costs for the first layer
of the defense.

Suppose we look at the situation later in the 1990s, when
the United States may be sending satellites into orbit
equipped with lasers, neutral particle beams or other more advanced and more effective devices. The lasers and particle
beams on these satellites will be more expensive equipment
than the "smart bullets" on the earlier generation of defensive
satellites, and the satellites that carry them are expected to

cost about $1 billion each. Calculations carried out by scientists at Livermore Laboratory show that, on the average, each satellite equipped with a "standard" laser* can destroy 23 Soviet SS-18 missiles costing a total of about $2.3 billion. That means that for every billion-dollar satellite we add to our defenses, the Soviets must spend $2.3 billion to counter that satellite. Once again, the ratio of marginal costs works strongly against the Soviet attacker seeking to overwhelm our defense.

So the bottom line is that whether we look at the lump-sum expenditures for the initial reaction to a defense, or at the marginal costs, the ratio of costs heavily favors the defense over the offense. This would be true for the Soviet response to an American "Star Wars" defense, or the American reaction to a Soviet "Star Wars" defense.

No development could be more favorable to the cause of ending the nuclear arms race and eliminating nuclear weapons from the world. For the meaning of these results is that if both the U.S. and USSR put a defense against missiles in place, neither country will be able to overwhelm the other's defense by building more missiles, and both nations must then recognize the futility of a continued competition in the building of offensive weapons of mass destruction.

---

*Twenty million watts of power focused by a thirty-foot mirror.

THE GALOSH. The Galosh, shown above in a May Day Parade in Red Square, is a key element in the operational missile defense system protecting Moscow. The ABM treaty allows the U.S. and the USSR each to protect one city.

Because the Galosh is not a ''smart'' missile, it may miss its target by more than a mile. Consequently it needs a large nuclear weapon—with an explosive power of more than one megaton—to make its kill.

The Soviet Union is improving its missile defenses around Moscow with a two-layer defense and better models of the Galosh. The first layer would intercept American warheads at very high altitudes, above the atmosphere. The second layer uses rockets that accelerate rapidly to full speed and can intercept a warhead at lower altitudes. This layer catches the warheads that leak through the first layer.

12   Toward a Nuclear-Free World

Some time ago I had a conversation with a British journalist, who explained to me why some European leaders have been opposed to an American "Star Wars" defense against Soviet missile attacks. It would re-create "Fortress America," he said, because if the United States possessed a shield against Soviet missiles, American security would be decoupled from the security of Western Europe and we would be less inclined to go to war for our European allies if the Soviets attacked them.

But, I said, an American shield against Soviet missiles makes the United States less vulnerable to a Soviet nuclear attack, and strengthens the basic NATO strategy. NATO is counting on the United States to defend Europe with nuclear weapons, if the USSR attacks with tanks and planes. This American threat was credible when NATO was formed, but it no longer is, because the massive Soviet missile buildup now gives the USSR the power to destroy the United States with its own nuclear weapons in retaliation. But if we could protect our homeland against Soviet missiles, our nuclear umbrella over Western Europe would regain some of its earlier credibility.

Furthermore, I said, American missile defenses will be as effective against the SS-20s aimed at Western Europe as they are against the intercontinental missiles that threaten the United States.* So, if we put our defensive satellites into orbit to protect the United States against Soviet intercontinental missiles, those satellites will also protect Europe against the SS-20s. When some of our satellites are "on station" over the USSR, others will be "on station" over Western Europe, guarding our allies against a Soviet missile attack.

Yes, the journalist said, but when you Americans build your missile defense, the Soviets will feel obliged to build one, too. Then you will both be safe from one another's missiles. Missiles will disappear from the strategic balance, and the Soviets will be free to invade Western Europe with conventional arms.

In other words, the journalist was saying, we Europeans need nuclear weapons. They give us security, and you Americans had better not use your technology to make them useless.

This exchange of views revealed a surprising fact. Many people, including prominent government leaders, see a positive value in keeping nuclear weapons, because they feel these weapons have kept World War III from breaking out. At any rate, they see no hope of getting rid of them. Prime Minister Thatcher has said about nuclear weapons: "The fact is we have had peace in Europe...for forty years. That is a very long period

---

*In one respect SS-20s are harder to shoot down than long-range missiles: their flight times are shorter, which gives our defense less time in which to fire at them. However, this disadvantage to the defense is more than compensated by features of the SS-20s that simplify our defense against them. First and most important, SS-20s travel at lower altitudes than long-range missiles, and therefore stay in the dense air of the lower atmosphere longer, which makes it easier for our defense to distinguish between the warheads and the decoys. The point here is that decoys, being lighter, are more retarded by air drag. Second, SS-20s, being small missiles compared to giants like the SS-18, have a relatively small payload. That means they carry fewer warheads and also fewer decoys. This again, simplifies the problem for our defense. Finally, SS-20s and other medium-range missiles travel more slowly than long-range missiles, which means they can be tracked more easily and the weapons to destroy them can be aimed with greater accuracy.

of peace. We are going to have to live with [the nuclear balance of terror] for a considerable period of time."[*][†]

Other people do not have as positive a feeling about nuclear weapons, but also do not see how to eliminate them. A distinguished group of Harvard faculty members has written: "Humanity has no alternative but ... to live in the world we know: a world of nuclear weapons ... Living with nuclear weapons is our only hope."[**]

But is that really so? Must we live with this curse forever? Jonathan Schell has thought long and hard about this question, and has reasoned his way to an important conclusion.[††] Today there is a nuclear balance between the two superpowers, with 10,000 intercontinental nuclear weapons in round numbers, in each arsenal.[§] But an equally effective balance would exist if each country had 5000 such weapons. And because of the enormous destructive power of these weapons, there would still be an effective nuclear balance if each country had only 1000 such weapons; or if each had 500, or 100. Such is the fearsome power of these weapons, that if each country had only 10 nuclear weapons, a nuclear balance would still exist. And if

---

[*] New York Times, December 23, 1984.

[†] Randall Forsberg has analyzed the view that nuclear weapons play a positive role, in a very clear and informative article in *World Policy Journal*, Vol. I, No. 2, Winter, 1984. She writes, "....most people subconsciously judge, I believe, that if nuclear weapons were suddenly abolished, aggression of the type that occurred before and during World War II might once again become common. Thus fear of large-scale conventional military aggression remains the most powerful argument for preserving [the nuclear weapon] and the greatest obstacle to doing away with it."

[**] *Living with Nuclear Weapons* by A. Carnesale, P. Doty, S. Hoffmann, S. P. Huntington, J. S. Nye, Jr. and S. G. Sagan, with a foreword by D. Bok, published by Bantam Books, New York, 1983.

[††] *The Abolition* by Jonathan Schell, Alfred A. Knopf, New York, 1984.

[§] The United States has approximately 7800 nuclear weapons that could be directed against the Soviet homeland. The USSR has at least 11,000 similar weapons that could be directed against the United States, according to information released by the Department of Defense in 1985.

10 weapons would deter an attack and keep the nuclear balance, then why not five or one—*or zero*? The deterring effect of nuclear weapons on aggression is effective all the way down to zero weapons, provided both sides have equal numbers of these weapons at every stage.

So, if a defense against missiles is in place on both sides, it is not necessary to have large nuclear arsenals to deter aggression. In fact, it is not necessary to have any arsenals; a world with no nuclear weapons will still be in a state of nuclear balance.

But suppose one side cheats after nuclear weapons are abolished. Suppose one side keeps a small number of these weapons concealed; or suppose after all nuclear weapons have been destroyed, one side secretly constructs a small number of new weapons. This would be a very effective stratagem for a would-be aggressor. In a world with no nuclear weapons, one weapon is king. How do we deal with the cheater in a nuclear-free world?

The new technologies of missile defense provide the answer. A defense sized to meet today's massive nuclear threat—thousands of warheads launched simultaneously—can counter the limited threat posed by the cheater—one, or a dozen, or a hundred warheads—with 100-percent effectiveness. When defenses are in place, cheating offers no reward in a nuclear-free world.*

---

*It is sometimes suggested that defenses against ballistic missiles would not be effective against the cruise missile—an exceedingly small, readily concealed, pilotless jet aircraft, that would presumably be hard to detect in flight. However this is not correct. The problem of detecting a cruise missile is different from the detection of a ballistic missile or its warheads, but not harder. Cruise missiles are larger than warheads, and will be visible to heat-sensitive detectors as well as radars. Stealth technology, useful as a countermeasure to ground radars, is not as useful against the space-based radars in a missile defense.

The slow speed of the cruise missile greatly simplifies the remaining steps in the defense. A missile defense sized to handle a simultaneous attack by thousands of warheads and tens of thousands of decoys, all moving at speeds in the neighborhood of 10,000 miles an hour, will find it an easy task to shoot down a cruise missile traveling at 550 miles an hour—the speed of a commer-

But how do we get there from here? Negotiations aimed at large reductions in the nuclear arsenals of the U.S. and USSR have been going on for a number of years, but they have not succeeded. Tension and insecurity have relentlessly driven the arsenals of the two powers upward to higher levels. Can we reverse course without jeopardizing national security?

This is the second major significance of the new technologies of missile defense. They can impart to the governments of the U.S. and the USSR the confidence needed to take that critical first step toward nuclear disarmament. Suppose the Soviets have 10,000 warheads in their arsenal, and suppose we have a defense that is 80 percent effective. That means we can shoot down 8000 of the 10,000 Soviet warheads, and only 2000 will reach their targets in the United States. But if the Soviets can only get 2000 warheads to the United States, we do not need 10,000 warheads to preserve the nuclear balance; we only need 2000, and we can destroy the rest.

So now we have a defense, and we have 2000 nuclear warheads. The Soviets have 10,000 warheads, but because of our defense, 8000 of those will be wasted if they are launched. Why should the Soviets keep the 8000 warheads, and the expensive missiles that carry them? Why not build down to 2000 warheads—*and put in a defense?* Then the United States and the Soviet Union each will have a defense, and a smaller arsenal— and the nuclear balance will still be preserved. The build-down process will have commenced.

Of course, when we take the critical first step toward a reduction of nuclear weapons, we will not necessarily want to

cial airliner. Even if the cruise missile is launched from a submarine off U.S. shores, it will take at least 10 minutes to reach its destination—ample time for our defenses to be effective against such a slow-moving object.

Space lasers, contrary to some views that have been expressed, are effective against the low-flying cruise missile, because a laser beam, being a ray of light, penetrates to the ground. Clouds offer a temporary screen against a space-based laser, but a cover of clouds is not likely to exist all the way to the target. (Bombers are even more vulnerable to lasers, since they fly above the clouds for hours on the way to their targets.)

destroy all our 8000 warheads at one time. That could leave us vulnerable, because the other side might put in a defense—*and not destroy any of their warheads.* Then the nuclear balance would be badly upset, and in a way that would be very dangerous for us. But if we had a good defense, we could afford to make a unilateral gesture—say, the destruction of 1000 warheads—without significant damage to our security.* And we would encourage the other side to put in a defense at the same time, and reduce its arsenal by 1000 warheads, as we had done. And so we would proceed together toward the abolition of nuclear weapons, in a stepwise, carefully phased, simultaneous reduction of the two arsenals, without compromise to the security of either nation.

So the process starts, and leads to the abolition of nuclear weapons, that can be undertaken once a defense is in place. The next step, and the one after that, and all that follow down to the end—the abolition—require continuing cooperation between the two nations, in carefully negotiated and parallel deployments of defenses, alternating with the incremental reduction of the two arsenals of destruction. That is the road to a nuclear-free world.

*This avenue to nuclear arms reduction has been discussed by Gregory Fossedal in the context of the Geneva arms control negotiations, in "The Reagan Doctrine," *The American Spectator*, Vol. 8, No. 3, March 1985, pp. 12–15.

Notes

Notes

CHAPTER 1

Page 1: The ABM Treaty was signed at Moscow on May 26, 1972. It entered into force October 3, 1972. The language quoted in the text is taken from Article VI(b) of the Treaty:

> "b) not to deploy in the future radars for early warning of strategic ballistic missile attack except locations along the periphery of its national territory and oriented outward."

Other articles spell out technical details of the restrictions on ABM activities. Article V-1 states:

> "Each Party undertakes not to develop, test, or deploy ABM systems or components which are sea-based, air-based, space-based, or mobile land-based."

Article XII, given below, specifies that neither nation shall interfere with attempts by the other to gain information needed to verify compliance with the treaty.

> "1. For the purpose of providing assurance of compliance with the provisions of this Treaty, each Party shall use national technical means of verification at its disposal in a manner consistent with generally recognized principles of international law.

"2. Each Party undertakes not to interfere with the national technical means of verification of the other Party operating in accordance with paragraph 1 of this Article.

"3. Each Party undertakes not to use deliberate concealment measures which impede verification by national technical means of compliance with the provisions of this Treaty. This obligation shall not require changes in current construction, assembly, conversion, or overhaul practices."

Part 2 of Article XV is also of special importance. It specifies:

"2. Each Party shall, in exercising its national sovereignty, have the right to withdraw from this Treaty if it decides that extraordinary events related to the subject matter of this Treaty have jeopardized its supreme interests. It shall give notice of its decision to the other Party six months prior to withdrawal from the Treaty. Such notice shall include a statement of the extraordinary events the notifying Party regards as having jeopardized its supreme interests."

Appended to the treaty is also the so-called "unilateral statement" entered into the record on May 9, 1972 by Ambassador Smith. This statement is excerpted as a footnote at the beginning of Chapter 2. The full text is as follows:

"A. Withdrawal from the ABM Treaty. The U.S. Delegation has stressed the importance the U.S. Government attaches to achieving agreement on more complete limitations on strategic offensive arms, following agreement on an ABM Treaty and on an Interim Agreement on certain measures with respect to the limitation of strategic offensive arms. *The U.S. Delegation believes that an objective of the follow-on negotiations should be to constrain and reduce on a long-term basis threats to the survivability of our respective strategic retaliatory forces.* The USSR Delegation has also indicated that the objectives of SALT would remain unfulfilled without the achievement of an agreement providing for more complete limitations on strategic offensive arms. Both sides recognize that the initial agreements would be steps toward the achievement of more complete limitations on strategic arms. *If an agreement providing for more complete strategic offensive arms limitations were not achieved within five years, U.S. supreme interests could be jeopardized. Should that occur, it would constitute a basis for withdrawal from the ABM Treaty.* The U.S. does not wish to see such a situation occur, nor do we believe that the USSR does. It is because we wish to prevent such a situation that we emphasize the importance the U.S. Government attaches to achievement of more complete limitations on strategic offensive arms. The U.S. Executive will inform the Congress in connection with Congressional consideration of the ABM Treaty and the Interim Agreement of this statement of the U.S. position." (Author's italics.)

CHAPTER 2

Data on the Soviet and American strategic arsenals are compiled from the following sources: J. M. Collins and J. P. Olakas, *U.S.: Soviet Military Balance*, Congressional Research Service Report #83-1535 (1983); *The Military Balance 1981–1982*, International Institute for Strategic Studies, London (1981); *Soviet Military Power*, First Edition (September 1981), Second Edition (March 1983) and Third Edition (April 1984); *Nuclear Weapons Databook*, Volume I: U.S. Nuclear Forces and Capabilities, Thomas B. Cochran, William M. Arkin, and Milton M. Hoenig, Ballinger Publishing Company, Cambridge, Mass., 1984.

Survivability of land-based missiles is discussed in detail in "How To Assess The Survivability of U.S. ICMBs" by Bruce W. Bennett, The Rand Corporation, Rand publication R-2577-FF-R-2578-FF, June 1980. See also "All You Ever Wanted To Know About MIRV and ICBM Calculations But Were Not Cleared to Ask" by L. E. Davis and W. R. Schilling, *Journal of Conflict Resolution*, Vol. 17, No. 2, June 1973. More general and very readable accounts can be found in "The Accuracy of Strategic Missiles" by Kosta Tsipis, *Scientific American*, July 1975 and "The Uncertainties of a Preemptive Nuclear Attack" by Matthew Bunn and Kosta Tsipis, *Scientific American*, November 1983.

The following sources provide a clear account of the communications links—the so-called Strategic Command, Control, Communications and Intelligence network or C³I—that would translate a presidential decision to release our missiles into operational reality. These sources also contain discussions of the critically important matter of vulnerability of our C³I network to a Soviet nuclear first strike: *The Command and Control of Nuclear Forces* by Paul Bracken, Yale University Press, New Haven, 1983; "Strategic Command, Control, Communications, and Intelligence" by Charles A. Zraker, *Science*, June 22, 1984, pp. 1306–1311; "The Command and Control of Nuclear War" by Ashton B. Carter, *Scientific American*, January 1985, pp. 32–39; "Go-Codes from Out There: Space Communications for World War III" by Thomas Karas, *Technology Illustrated*, March 1983, pp. 33–40; "Strategic Command and Control: America's Achilles Heel?" by Jonathan B. Tucker, *Technology Review*, August/September 1983, pp. 36–49, 74–76.

Page 19. Launch of SS-20s over the polar region; *National Security Record*, 1984, p. 3, The Heritage Foundation, Washington, D.C.

Page 20. Statement by General Vessey on Minuteman vulnerability: *New York Times*, May 6, 1983.

Page 21. Penetration of Soviet airspace by B-52s: *Soviet Military Power*, March 1983, p. 26.

Page 23. Non-acoustic detection of submerged submarines: *Military Space*, October 15, 1984, p. 3.

Page 26. "Suicide or surrender:" Henry Kissinger, *Years of Upheaval*, p. 256, Little, Brown and Company, Boston, 1982.

CHAPTER 3

Page 38. General Vessey on Launch On Warning: *New York Times*, May 6, 1983.

Page 40. Soviet leadership bunkers: *Soviet Military Power*, April 1984, p. 41.

CHAPTER 4

Statements attributed to the Union of Concerned Scientists are taken from *Space-Based Missile Defense*, A report by the Union of Concerned Scientists, Cambridge, Mass. 1984; and *The Fallacy of Star Wars*, Vintage Books, New York. Statements attributed to a report prepared for the OTA are taken from *Directed Energy Missile Defense in Space*: A Background paper by Ashton Carter, Office of Technology Assessment, April 1984.

The Livermore computations on the number of laser-equipped satellites required for a defensive screen are described in "Critique of Systems Analysis in the OTA Study," by Christopher T. Cunningham, Lawrence Livermore National Laboratory, Livermore, California, Report No. DDV-84-0007.

The Los Alamos critique of the report to the OTA is contained in the following Los Alamos unclassified memorandum: "Comments on the OTA Paper on Directed Energy Missile Defense in Space," G. Canavan, H. Flicker, O. Judd, and K. Taggart, Los Alamos National Laboratory, Los Alamos, New Mexico, May 6, 1984.

Page 40. Report to the Department of Defense on the feasibility of missile defense: *Ballistic Missile Defense and U.S. National Security: A Summary Report*, prepared for the Future Security Strategy Study, October 1983. See also *The Strategic Defense Initiative*, Statement by Dr. James C. Fletcher Before the House Committee on Armed Services, March 1984.

Page 49. Downward revision to 162 satellites: "Missile-Killing Potential of Satellite Constellations" by Richard Garwin, December 30, 1984.

Page 50. Weight of a neutral particle beam accelerator: *Space-Based Missile Defense*, p. 102.

Page 52. Weight of a lead shield against the neutral particle beam: Office of Technology Assessment report, pp. 30, 50.

CHAPTER 5

A brief account of the law of gravity and the dynamics of satellite orbits can be found in *Astronomy: Fundamentals and Frontiers* by Robert Jastrow and Malcolm H. Thompson, John Wiley and Sons, New York, 1984. See also *The Promise of Space* by Arthur C. Clarke, Harper and Row, New York, 1968. Descriptions of the Soviet space program and Soviet military satellites can be found in *The Battle for Space* by Curtis Peebles, Beaufort Books, Inc., New York, 1983, and in *The Soviet Year in Space*, 1983 by Nicholas L. Johnson, Teledyne Brown Engineering, Colorado Springs. Interesting information regarding military uses of satellites in early warning, reconnaissance and communication can be found in the sources listed in these Notes for Chapter 2, relating to the U.S. strategic command, control and communications network.

Page 58. Photography from satellites: "The Keyhole Satellite Program" by Jeffrey Richelson, *The Journal of Strategic Studies* (June, 1984), pp. 123–151.

Page 61. Rehearsal for nuclear war; Peebles, pp. 120–121.

Pages 64–66. Satellite vulnerability: *US Space System Survivability: Strategic Alternatives for the 1990s* by Robert B. Giffen, National Security Affairs Monograph Series 82–4, National Defense University Press, Fort Lesley J. McNair, Washington, DC, 1982; *Military Space*, September 3 and 17, 1984.

CHAPTER 6

The best source of information on Robert Goddard's early rocket experiments is found in *The Papers of Robert H. Goddard*, Volumes I–III, edited by Esther C. Goddard and G. Edward Pendray, McGraw-Hill, New York, 1970. A very readable account can be found in *This High Man* The Life of Robert H. Goddard by Milton Lehman, Farrar, Straus and Company, New York, 1968; also *Space* by Patrick Moore, the Natural History Press, Garden City, New York, 1969.

Accounts of the early German experiments and the development of the V-2 can be found in Moore and in *Rockets, Missiles, and Men in Space* by Willy Ley, The Viking Press, New York, 1968.

Page 72. Soviet warheads: Updated figures released by the Department of Defense are in *The New York Times*, March 21, 1985.

CHAPTER 7

General discussions of the laser can be found in *Lasers* by Jeff Hecht, and Dick Teresi, Ticknor & Fields, New York, 1983, and *Beam Weapons* by Jeff Hecht, Plenum Press, New York, 1984. *Principles of Lasers* by Orazio Svelto, Plenum Press, New York, 1976, contains a more technical discussion. The invention of the laser was described by Charles H. Townes in *Science 84*, November 1984, pp. 153–155.

A very interesting article on new methods of compensating for the spreading effect of the atmosphere on a laser beam, as well as the effect of imperfections in the laser and associated optics, is contained in "Through the Looking Glass with Phase Conjugation" by B. J. Feldman, I. J. Bigio, R. A. Fisher, C. R. Phipps, Jr., D. E. Watkins, and

S. J. Thomas, *Los Alamos Science*, Fall 1982, pp. 2–18. See also, "Adaptive Optics Correct Laser Beams" by Jeff Hecht, *High Technology*, September 1984.

Innovations in the design of large telescope mirrors are discussed in *Astronomy: Fundamentals and Frontiers*, pp. 98–102.

CHAPTER 8

The electromagnetic railgun is described in *Aviation Week and Space Technology*, December 5, 1983, pp. 62-63; see also *Military Space*, October 15, 1984, pp. 4–5 and *IEEE Spectrum*, April 1982, pp. 30–36.

Brief descriptions of the x-ray laser are contained in *Aviation Week and Space Technology*, February 23, 1981, pp. 25–27 and *Nature*, July 9, 1981, p. 108 and July 19, 1984, p. 180.

CHAPTER 9

Page 105. Test of the "smart bullet" concept: *Aviation Week and Space Technology*, June 18, 1984, pp. 19-20 and October 29, 1984, pp. 23-24.

CHAPTER 10

Information related to the material in this chapter can be found in "The Technologies for Ballistic Missile Defense" by James C. Fletcher, *Issues in Science and Technology*, National Academy of Sciences, Washington, DC, Fall 1984, pp. 13–29.

CHAPTER 11

Information regarding Soviet missile defenses and "Star Wars" research can be found in reports and testimony by James C. Fletcher listed in these Notes under Chapter 4. See also, *Aviation Week and*

Space Technology, August 29, 1983, p. 19 and "Soviets Accelerate Missile Defense Efforts," by Clarence A. Robinson, Jr., *Aviation Week and Space Technology*, January 16, 1984, pp. 14–16.

For reports on the Soviet radar at Abalakova and its ABM significance, see "U.S. Scrutinizing New Soviet Radar" by Philip J. Klass, *Aviation Week and Space Technology*, August 22, 1983; *Soviet Military Power*, April 1984, p. 33; "U.S. Experts Condemn Soviet Radar" by R. Jeffrey Smith, *Science*, March 22, 1985, pp. 1442–1444.

Page 127. Soviet Spending on strategic defense exceeds its expenditures on offense: Caspar W. Weinberger, remarks to the Foreign Press Center, December 19, 1984.

Appendices

Appendix 1:
Accurate Warheads
and the Nuclear First Strike

Just as the defense now has its "smart bullet" that can steer itself into an oncoming missile or warhead, the offense has its "smart warhead" that steers itself into the target with deadly accuracy.

A highly accurate, smart warhead can carry only a very small charge of nuclear explosive and still accomplish its military tasks. When the amount of nuclear explosive is small, radioactive fallout from the explosion will also be small, and the nuclear weapon can be used to achieve precisely defined military objectives, without mass civilian casualties.

In the future, the smart ICBM warhead, equipped with electronic brains and infrared or radar "eyes," will hitch a ride to the general vicinity of the target on its ICBM bus; then, disembarking, it will steer itself into a particular spot on the target within a yard or two to accomplish its task with nice precision. This development opens up major new possibilities for the military planner. A very small Soviet nuclear weapon, carried across the ocean by an ICBM, guides itself down the smokestack of the Consolidated Edison plant in New York; an American warhead, carried 5000 miles in the nose of an ICBM, drops down onto a critical transformer in the Moscow power grid; a bridge is destroyed by a small nuclear explosive charge, ferried across oceans and continents on an ICBM and carefully placed at the foot of a pier; a small nuclear charge is delivered to the door of a Minuteman or an SS-18 silo; exploding, it crushes the silo door, destroying the missile. It is not necessary to crush the entire silo with the violence of a megaton blockbuster warhead; missiles are fragile, and gentler means suffice to disable them.

Command posts, ammunition dumps, highways, and airport runways—all are vulnerable to very small nuclear charges, skillfully targeted. Nearly every task allotted to today's terrible nuclear weapons can be accomplished in the future by missiles armed with small, smart warheads.*

The smart, highly accurate warhead means an end to the era of nuclear blockbusters. The history of the last twenty-five years bears this out; it shows that as the accuracy of American and Soviet ICBMs increased, their nuclear warheads became smaller, as the upper chart (*opposite*) shows. In the beginning, nuclear warheads carried by ICBMs were enormous, because they tended to come down wide of the mark and needed a large radius of destruction to accomplish their military tasks. But as the accuracy of American ICBMs improved, our nuclear warheads shrank to a small fraction of their original size. Today's warheads are one-seventh the size they were in 1960. My figures on the Soviet arsenal go back only ten years, but in that period Soviet warheads decreased in size by a factor of three. As a consequence of these trends, today the total destructive power, or megatonnage, of the American arsenal is one-quarter what it was in 1960 as the lower chart shows.**

This shrinkage in the total destructive power of nuclear weapons is the result of an improvement in missile accuracy from about one mile in the early 1960s to 300 yards in the 1970s and 150 yards today. When smart warheads are placed on ICBMs—which has not happened yet—ICBM accuracy will improve by a quantum leap. At that stage, the nuclear arsenals of the superpowers can be expected to decrease even more dramatically than they have in the past 25 years.

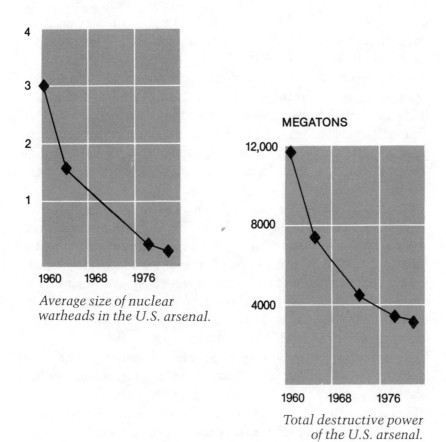

Average size of nuclear
warheads in the U.S. arsenal.

Total destructive power
of the U.S. arsenal.

*Trends in warhead accuracy and their implications are discussed by: "Improving Missile Accuracies" by James T. Westwood and Jason L. Feer, *National Defense*, July/August 1984; "When a Nuclear Strike is Thinkable" by Pierre Gallois and John Train, *The Wall Street Journal*, March 2, 1984; "From Arms Control to Controlled Security" by Zbigniew Brzezinski, *The Wall Street Journal*, July 10, 1984.

**Data compiled from the following sources: J. M. Collins and J. P. Olakas, *U.S.: Soviet Military Balance*, Congressional Research Service Report #83-1535 (1983); *The Military Balance 1981–1982*, International Institute for Strategic Studies, London (1981); A. Wohlstetter, United States Strategic Institute Report 75–1, Washington, D.C. (1975).

At first this may seem implausible, because presumably bigger bombs are better for the military planner. But large nuclear weapons are very undesirable from a military point of view. In fact, some experts believe they are not militarily usable at all. If exploded on the battlefield, nuclear weapons tend to contaminate the terrain with radioactivity and prevent the occupying troops from advancing. If employed in "surgical" ICBM attacks against military sites, they generate radioactive fallout that kills innocent civilians. If used in large numbers against cities, they stir up great clouds of poisonous dust that can roll back on the lands of the attacking army. And then, there is the specter of nuclear winter.

So, for all these reasons, if large nuclear weapons are not needed, they will not be used. For a time, the major powers may keep some blockbusters in reserve as a deterrent to genocidal missile attacks on their cities. But every truly military task that is assigned today to a megaton warhead—the destruction of a missile silo, a command post, an airfield or an ammunition dump—will be assigned in the future to a smart warhead carrying a very small charge of nuclear explosive.

This development has its good side and its bad side. The good side is that the danger of radioactive fallout diminishes to the vanishing point. The bad side is that the nuclear first strike—that most chilling prospect of modern times—becomes a feasible military option, for it can be used to inflict a total nuclear defeat on an adversary thousands of miles away, without massive civilian casualties or global damage to the environment. This major change in the strategic calculus—spawned again by technological advances—heightens the importance of replacing the strategy of Mutual Assured Destruction with the new strategy of Deterrence by Defense—a strategy that can make *any* nuclear first strike unattractive to an adversary.

The improvements in accuracy that have generated these revolutionary changes in thinking about nuclear weapons are very interesting if divorced from their deadly applications. How do they work? How do guided missiles guide themselves?

How does a smart warhead think? Take the missile first. A missile is entirely blind during most of its flight. Even if its warhead has eyes, they can be used only toward the end of the flight, just before impact. A missile in mid-flight is in the same situation as a blindfolded pilot trying to keep his plane on course. How would the pilot do that? He would try to use the same senses that alert a person dozing in a railway car to the fact that the train has started to move. That is, the pilot would feel the tug of inertia on his body when the plane veered to the left or right or went into a spin.

Of course, the pilot would not notice small changes in the speed and direction of the plane because his body's ability to sense these inertial effects would be rather limited. Yet such small changes, accumulating over minutes or hours, could add up to a fatal crash. Still, the idea is sound. If instruments existed that could measure the changes in speed and direction of the plane with great precision, and if the output from these instruments could be used to control the plane's flaps and rudder, it would fly a nearly perfect course. This method is, in fact, used today in airplanes, along with radio guidance, to control their course in blind flight.

The same method is used to control the flight of a missile. The instruments needed to make the measurements of the speed and direction of flight have been known for some time. Changes in the *speed* of the missile are measured by an accelerometer, which is, in essence, a spring with a weight attached to one end. If the spring is suddenly accelerated, the weight, which tends to resist changes in speed, lags behind and the spring is stretched. The degree of stretch in the spring indicates the amount of acceleration.

Changes in the *direction* of the missile's flight are measured by a gyroscope. The axis of a rapidly spinning gyroscope tends to maintain a fixed direction in space, regardless of what is going on around it. Suppose a gyroscope, mounted in a missile, has its axis pointed precisely in the direction of the missile's flight, and suppose then that the missile veers off course slightly, say to the left. If a person were riding blind inside the missile he would not be able to feel the slight change in direction, but he would see that the axis of the gyroscope had apparently shifted a little bit to the right. He would understand the meaning of this shift, namely, that the missile had actually veered to the left. If he wanted to, he could change the direction of the rocket motor to deflect the missile into the right path again. If no one is riding in the missile, as is normally the case, electrical connections can be run from the gyroscopes and accelerometers to the rocket motor to do the same thing.

This system, called inertial guidance, has been developed to a high degree of refinement in ICBMs. The newest version, which has been installed in MX missiles, is responsible for the 150-yard accuracy of the MX warhead.

Can we expect further improvements in missile accuracy in the future? Probably not from inertial guidance. The biggest problem in inertial guidance is the tendency of the gyroscope to drift, or change its direction slowly. A drift rate as modest as one-hundredth of a degree per hour can cause an error of 500 yards in the aim of an ICBM. Other problems, such as small variations in the earth's gravity and the action of rain or snow on the reentering warhead, add to the error. According to missile experts, the 150-yard accuracy of the MX warhead is close to the limit that can be achieved with inertial guidance and ordinary or "dumb" warheads. The reason is that once an ordinary warhead gets off course, it stays off course. It has no way of looking around, taking its bearings, and making a course correction.

But that is not the end of the story if the missile is equipped with a "smart" warhead. After the accelerometers and gyroscopes on the missile have done their job, and all the rocket motors have shut down, the warhead separates from the burned-out rocket (or from the bus containing several warheads, if the missile is MIRVed) and continues on its way under the force of gravity alone, in a trajectory curving up, over and down again. As the warhead comes down, its computer enters the picture. Acting as the warhead's brain, the computer studies the information on the location of the target provided by the "eye" of the warhead—which is either a radar or a heat-sensitive detector—and then figures out how the warhead should change its direction to score a bull's-eye hit.

How can an artificial eye and brain do that? The answer is: Not too differently from the human eye and brain. Compare the warhead's performance to the interplay of the eye and brain in the simple act of steering a car. A person doing that must look out the window and compare what the eye sees with an image stored in the brain's memory or printed on a road map. The warhead goes through the same steps, although the details differ. When it is about 50,000 feet above the target, and descending rapidly, a shroud covering the warhead's nose is jettisoned to reveal a radar antenna. The radar antenna rotates rapidly, 120 times a minute. As it rotates, it sends out a radar which sweeps across the terrain below, like the beam from a revolving searchlight. The moving radar beam illuminates the entire target with radar waves. Some of the waves bounce back to the radar antenna. The antenna collects and focuses the radar waves from the different parts of the terrain to form an image, just as a camera lens collects and focuses light into an image.

The result is a radar "picture" of the scene. The parts of the scene that reflect radar waves strongly show up as bright spots in the "picture." Other parts, which absorb radar waves without reflecting them, show up as dark spots in the "picture." Plowed fields and rough ground, for example, show up as bright regions. Metal rooftops appear very bright. Vegetation usually appears moderately bright or gray. Smoothly paved roads and airport runways usually appear black, even if covered with light-colored concrete, because the radar beam bounces off them in the forward direction as if they were mirrors, and is not reflected back to the antenna.

In the radar image formed in this way, landmarks like fields, roads and large buildings usually stand out clearly through the contrast of their bright and dark regions. This radar image, which looks like a black and white television picture, is read into the warhead's computer memory and stored there. It is the approaching warhead's view of the target area.

The warhead's computer has another image stored in it, which reveals the scene the radar should see if the warhead is exactly on course and aimed precisely at the target. This image was prepared beforehand by the Defense Intelligence Agency from aircraft and satellite reconnaissance photographs. The same landmarks—fields, roads and so on—appear in both images. However, since the warhead is bound to be somewhat off course, the image of the target that was placed in the computer beforehand will not coincide exactly with the image perceived by the radar as the warhead approaches the ground. For example, if the target is a missile silo, the silo will be in the exact center of the stored image prepared by the Defense Intelligence Agency, but it will be off center in the image recorded by the warhead's radar.

Now the warhead's computer electronically slides one image over the other until the two images coincide. The computer is doing what people do when they hold two photographs of the same scene up to the light and slide one over the other until objects in the two photos match. The amount of north-south and east-west sliding that is necessary indicates how far off course the warhead is, and in which direction. Armed with this information, the computer then sends instructions to small motors controlling movable vanes at the rear of the warhead. The vanes, which are like the rudder and flaps on an airplane, adjust their positions to deflect the warhead into a path leading to a bull's-eye impact.

The 25-yard accuracy achieved in this way by the Pershing 2 warhead is only the beginning of a new revolution in missile accuracy. Later generations of smart warheads, with more highly evolved brains, and eyes sensitive to visible and infrared wavelengths as well as radar, can be expected to deposit their explosive charges within yards or even feet of the target.

Appendix 2:
Countermeasures

Several methods have been proposed for countering a defense against missiles at relatively low cost. For example, the attacking nation could make the surface of its missiles very shiny, to reflect our laser beams. It is also possible to impart a spin to the missiles as they are launched, to spread the energy of the laser beam over the surface of the missile and dilute its effect by a factor of π, or roughly three. Another countermeasure would be a missile that accelerates to full speed very quickly—a so-called "fast-burn booster." The advantage here is that the fast-burn booster will burn out while still in the atmosphere. This could protect the booster from some of our most promising defenses, such as the neutral particle beam, which cannot penetrate into dense air.

The usefulness of these countermeasures depends partly on their inherent effectiveness, and partly on the penalty the attacker must pay to implement them. Consider the shine, for example. Putting a shine on a missile sounds like a useful suggestion, but would be ineffective in practice, because no shine is perfect; even if the shiny surface reflects 99 percent or more of the incident laser light, some laser energy is bound to get through and will heat the surface. The heating tends to dull the shine, so more heat gets through. This dulls the shine some more, and still more heats gets through...Very soon the shine is gone.

Another problem with shining up the missile is that during the launch it tends to get dirty, partly because of its own exhaust gases, and its luster is dulled. In addition, as the booster accelerates, it compresses and heats the air above it, and the plume of hot air sweeps downward around the side of the missile, oxidizing the surface, and also tending to take the shine away. Finally, the shine itself is obtained by applying a thin coat of reflective material to the missile, but the coating has a different coefficient of expansion from the metal skin underneath, and tends to buckle when the missile is heated by the laser beam. This leads to the catastrophic failure of the reflective layer.

A strippable outer coating has been proposed as a way of keeping the missile's surface clean during launch. The trouble with this suggestion is that the strippable coating, which is to be wrapped around the entire missile, must be quite thin, or it will weigh too much and force the attacker to eliminate several warheads from the missile's payload. The coating must also be sturdy, or air resistance will strip it away. And it must be heat-resistant, because the missile gets quite hot as it rises rapidly through the atmosphere. These requirements are partly contradictory, and reconciling them will not be easy. A substantial amount of development and testing would be necessary to make certain that such a device works well and does not interfere with reliable missile performance. And all this is for a very uncertain gain to the Soviets if they were to try it, because, as noted above, when the coating is stripped away and the shiny surface underneath is exposed to attack by our laser beam, the heat of the laser beam will degrade the shine rapidly.

Spinning the missile also sounds like a good idea. However, it does not gain the attacker anything if the laser energy is transmitted in sharp pulses that can catch the missile in one point of its spin, so to speak. The experts say there is no problem in building a laser that sends out its energy in sharp pulses.

The fast-burn booster is frequently mentioned as a very effective countermeasure to several kinds of missile defense. A fast-burn booster usually is described as a missile that burns out in 50 seconds, compared to three minutes for the MX or Minuteman, and five minutes for the SS-18. A missile that burns out in as short a time as 50 seconds would end its boost phase at an altitude of about 50 miles. The neutral particle beam, on the other hand, can penetrate down to an altitude of only about 70 miles before its effectiveness is destroyed by collisions with atoms in the atmosphere. The reason is that the atoms in the beam collide with atoms in the atmosphere and bounce around, which causes the beam to spread out in space. As a consequence, it is less intense when it strikes the target, and relatively ineffective. In addition, when the beam collides with atoms it sometimes knocks electrons out of them, which causes the beam to lose energy, further decreasing its effectiveness.

In spite of its potential for defeating the neutral particle beam, under more careful scrutiny the fast-burn booster appears to be less useful than it seemed at first. The principal problem with the fast-burn booster is that after it burns out, it must still deploy the bus containing the warheads. But the neutral particle beam is just as effective against the bus and its warheads after the boost phase. If the beam penetrates the electronics of the bus at an early stage, while most of the warheads are still on board, we catch nearly all the warheads in one shot, and the results are almost as good for our defense as destroying the missile would have been.

That means the attacker, who has protected his missile against our neutral particle beam by having the missile burn out quickly, still has to worry about protecting the bus. This can be done by having the bus deploy its warheads—that is, push them off into space—while the bus is still within the atmosphere and safe from our beam. However, if the Soviets, for example, were to do that, they would pay a very serious penalty because the warheads would be subject to air drag, which would seriously degrade their accuracy. This would have disastrous consequences for Soviet hopes of destroying our hardened military targets and crippling our retaliatory force.

The Soviets could overcome that problem also, by giving every warhead its own guidance and steering rockets, so that the warhead could change its course to compensate for the effects of air drag, and preserve its accuracy. In other words, each warhead would ride on a bus of its own. But many small buses add up to more weight than one large bus. Because of the extra weight, the missile cannot carry as many warheads. According to calculations, the number of warheads would be reduced by a factor of two or more. But cutting the destructive power of the Soviet nuclear arsenal by a factor of two would itself be a major plus for the American defense.

Fast-burn boosters have other problems. A rocket that accelerates from a standing start to roughly 15,000 miles an hour in less than a minute presents horrendous technical problems to the missile designer. Fast-burn rockets tend to explode and are not reliable; they get very hot because they move through the atmosphere so rapidly; and their structure must be stiffened to protect them against the battering forces created by their own acceleration. This last point imposes an additional penalty on the payload of the "fast-burn" missile, because the weight of the heavier structure must be compensated by the loss of another quarter to a third of the missile's payload.

The bottom line is that the number or warheads carried by the fast-burn booster is likely to be a small fraction of the number carried by a normal missile of that size. That would make the fast-burn booster an extremely expensive missile in cost per warhead. And if the Soviets went to the time and expense of replacing all their missiles—a $500 billion investment—with these costly new ones, that might avail them nothing, because our neutral particle beam could still attack their warheads with great effectiveness during the long midcourse portion of the flight.

Another suggested countermeasure is a heavy coat of material, perhaps half an inch thick, spread over a missile to protect it from the laser beam. The heat of the laser beam vaporizes the protective coating but leaves the missile's surface beneath undamaged. The difficulty with this suggestion is that the weight of the protective coating is substantial. Since the missile must carry this extra burden upward against the pull of gravity, it must compensate for it by dropping some of its payload. If the coating were applied to an SS-18, for example, it would reduce the payload of that missile by three to four tons, which is approximately equal to the total weight of the 10 warheads on the SS-18. In other words protecting SS-18s by this countermeasure would reduce the usefulness of that missile to zero.

The "space mine," still another method for foiling a defense against missiles, has received serious study by defense scientists. The space mine is a small, silent satellite, perhaps equipped with stealth technologies to make it invisible to radar, that shadows one of our laser-equipped satellites, ready to move in and blow it up on command.

The trouble with this idea, as with several other promising suggestions for countering a missile defense, is that it does not take into account the effect of atmospheric drag. Although the air through which a satellite moves is extremely thin, nonetheless, it exerts a resisting force on the satellite. This force, or atmospheric drag, varies from one satellite to another. As a result of differences in the amount of atmospheric drag, our laser-equipped satellite and the space mine will tend to draw apart over the course of many orbits, even if they were close together initially. To stay close to our satellite, the Soviet space mine must fire a small rocket now and then. But every time the space mine fires a rocket, it makes its presence known to the American satellite by the heat and light of the rocket flame. When that happens, our satellites, being armed hostile objects, will fire at the space mine and destroy it. If our laser-equipped satellites do not carry suitable weapons for this purpose, other satellites in the defensive system, which have been assigned the task of armed escorts, will do the job.

It may be possible for the space mine to shield its rocket exhaust from the eyes of the satellite it is tracking. However, the plans for the missile defense call for a network of surveillance satellites that will be looking at the intruder from several directions. The space mine may be able to conceal the flame of its exhaust from some of the surveillance satellites, but it cannot conceal the flame from all simultaneously.

Of course, if the space mine stays at a respectful distance, our defense will have no reason to interfere with its activities. But if it makes an attempt to close in for the kill, we are bound to see it and can destroy it.

The balloon is another interesting proposal for defeating missile defenses. The idea here is that after the boost phase is over, and the booster rocket has fallen away, the bus that normally deploys the Soviet warheads will instead deploy a large number of "balloons." These balloons are light, metallized, hollow spheres. Some balloons will actually have warheads inside them, and some will not. Not knowing which balloons contain warheads, we will waste our midcourse defenses on killing every balloon in sight, empty or not. In effect, the Soviets will be playing a shell game.

Since the empty balloons are light in weight and many can be deployed, this Soviet countermeasure will greatly dilute the effectiveness of our midcourse defense. If the balloon is many-layered, so that when a burst from one of our laser breaks the outermost balloon another is revealed inside, then the dilution of our defenses is even greater.

The trouble with this idea is that we can tell quite easily which balloons have warheads and which do not. The method is the same as the one described in Chapter 10 for discriminating decoys from genuine warheads. We need only tap the balloons, in effect, by directing a relatively weak pulse of laser energy at them and then observing their recoil. The empty balloons will recoil more rapidly than the loaded ones.

The Soviets couild defeat our testing method by making their balloons heavy, so that they would all recoil in about the same way, whether or not they contained warheads. But if the balloons are heavy, they take up weight that would otherwise be allotted to warheads. In that case the Soviets may as well throw the balloons overboard and use warheads instead.

A group of American scientists has proposed still another stratagem for countering our defense—one that depends on a relocation of the Soviet missiles and silos, rather than a technical ploy. This proposal is based on calculations which show that if all the missiles in a mass Soviet attack are launched in a cluster from one small area—the so-called "point" launch—the number of satellites needed to shoot down these missiles becomes considerable greater. The increase in the number of satellites is quite large—about a factor of three. This could make the cost of our defense quite expensive—remembering, again, that the cost of each satellite is about one billion dollars.

But is it conceivable that the Soviet Union would ever cluster all its missiles tightly together in one spot? For several reasons, it would not. For one thing, if all the missiles are located in one spot, and all are launched at one time, the times of arrival at their various targets in the United States will be widely different. That means the Soviets cannot effect a surprise attack that would take out all at once our command structure, airfields, submarine bases, and missile silos, since these military sites are located at widely different flight times from any single place in the USSR. Suppose the Soviets try to overcome this handicap by launching their missiles over an extended period of time, so as to achieve a simultaneous arrival at the various targets. Then our defense becomes enormously more effective, because it can pick off the Soviet missiles one by one as they rise from their silos.

The point launch would create other problems for an attacker. If the Soviet Union, for example, were to launch from one location at one time, all its warheads and decoys would be bunched tightly together as they coursed through space. This would reduce the time needed to slew around from one warhead to another during the midcourse phase of the defense and, again, greatly increase the effectiveness of our defense. It would also make the warheads ideal targets for the x-ray laser.

Finally, putting all the Soviet missiles in one place increases the effectiveness of our terminal defense as well, because it then becomes difficult for the Soviets to "ladder down". That refers to a technique for foiling a terminal defense in which the attacker explodes a nuclear weapon far above the missile silo or other target to create a fireball that will blind the ground radars on which our terminal defense depends. The fireball clears the way for another nuclear weapon that explodes and creates a fireball farther down, which clears the way for still another warhead, and so on, until finally the last warhead, swimming through these fireballs, reaches the target. But laddering down is impossible if all the missiles are in one place, unless they are launched at different times, and that is, as noted, disadvantageous to the Soviets for other reasons.

All in all, the last thing the Soviets are likely to do in response to our defense is to place their entire fleet of new missiles at one location.

Picture Credits

Index

171